Emah I...

Sooside Memories

by

Danny Gill

Copyright © 2016 Danny Gill

All rights reserved, including the right to reproduce this book, or portions thereof in any form. No part of this text may be reproduced, transmitted, downloaded, decompiled, reverse engineered, or stored, in any form or introduced into any information storage and retrieval system, in any form or by any means, whether electronic or mechanical without the express written permission of the author.

ISBN: 978-1-326-56896-2

All the proceeds from my book will go to the fund set up to get a statue built to the memory of "World Champion Boxer Benny Lynch".

Danny Gill.

Benny Lynch came from the Gorbals. His early years were tough but he came from a community who saw his talent and helped him nurture it. He fought his way from the streets to the ring and in turn conquered the world.

He became World Champion in 1935 and brought the title back to Scotland to enormous crowds of over 100,000 people who were waiting at Glasgow's Central Station. Benny was known all over the world and some say he was the best fighter they ever saw in the ring.

Sadly Benny died in his early thirties, and though he is still remembered with pride and great affection, he has never had a lasting memorial to honour him.

We are trying to raise money for a statue which will be placed in Glasgow in Benny's memory, and any help would be gratefully received as we have a lot of money to raise, but we know we can do it for the "Little King" of the Gorbals. Let's do this for Benny!

Foreword

In this book I have tried to take us on a walk down memory lane with everyday experiences that we all shared when living in that era of the old tenements in the soo side, and later on in the multi story blocks of flats and low rise houses which all took the place of the tenements.

So, from "midgie rakin" to playing all our many games in the streets or "gaun over the toon" to visit Lewis's store in Argyle Street etc I hope these memories take us all back to the times when we all lived in that close knit community.

Then later thousands of us, including myself, were shipped out to the new housing schemes that were being built on the outskirts of Glasgow. Although these new housing schemes were to be our new homes with an inside toilet and bath, it just wasn't the same (in my view) as living in the soo side where we had grown up knowing everyone up our close and closes near and far.

Who can forget taking a walk over to Saltmarket and Paddy's market or the Barras, and even if you never bought anything it was just a great experience visiting them.

I know many books have been written about the Gorbals and I must say that I personally love reading them all. In a hundred years from now and more people will still be reading them and wanting to know how we got on in our everyday lives living in the soo side, so here in my book I have tried to do this.

Of course people of my generation will know exactly what we all did back in the day, but I want not only to refresh their memories, but to explain to a new generation of people what we all did so they too can share our memories.

So with my poems, chapters of my book, Glasgow jokes and a few photos, I hope you can come with me on a walk down memory lane because for me it was a truly great experience living in those days. Times were hard but as I have often said in the past "We had nothing, but we had everything."

Acknowledgements

Firstly, I would like to thank my good friend Josephine (Josey) O'Boyle for giving me great assistance in preparing my book, "Emah Roo." My book would not have been finished as quick if it hadn't been for the great help that Josey gave me, so once again thank you so very much Josey.

I would also like to thank Mrs Jane Hardie Robertson from Seath Street, Govanhill, Glasgow whose son kindly allowed me to use his photos in my book, I am much indebted to you both and thank you once again.

A debt of gratitude goes to my parents, grandparents, friends and neighbours for their love and kindness when I was a wean growing up in the soo side, for without them I would not have been able to write this book.

Thanks also go to David and Gwen at PublishNation who published my book for me and thank you for answering all my questions in the process.

Last, but not least, I would like to thank every one of you who has taken the time to read my book "Emah Roo" and I do hope you enjoyed it.

Thank you, Danny Gill.

Author's note

Last year when I wrote my book "Gorbals and Oatlands" I completely forgot to insert two stories, one from Marilyn Hamilton about the Gorbals and one from Colin Mackie about Oatlands. I did apologise to them both profusely for omitting their stories and hope I can make amends by printing their stories now in this book.

Marilyn Hamilton nee McGonigle

I would like to tell you about my wee family the McGonigles, and our memorable life being brought up in the Gorbals. My mum is Esther McGonigle and my dad Willie McGonigle. They had four daughters Marilyn, Carol, Marie and Susan. The six of us lived one up in a room and kitchen with an outside toilet at 363 Lawmoor Street until we moved to what we thought was "Hollywood," the flats at Queen Elizabeth Square.

Our house was the 'Showhouse' at A1 Queen Elizabeth Square, one up with the huge verandah at the end near the Rose Garden. We went from sharing a room and kitchen to a three bedroomed house with kitchen, living room, bathroom and hot water. We thought we had died and gone to heaven.

My mum used to stand and watch her big washing blowing out in the verandah whereas back in Lawmoor Street the washing hung out the window on a pole above the windowsill with the milk and butter to keep fresh and the four pairs of sand shoes whitened and the middens down below. No matter where we lived or what we had or didn't have, we were well looked after, loved and happy. I and my three sisters all went to St Francis Primary School with our brown and gold uniforms. New shoes for Easter and full rig-out for the First Sunday in May.

The four of us were married in the beautiful St Francis Chapel with a scramble on the pavement outside.

My dad was a character who worked in Dixon Blazes and loved the pub. He would regularly bring back stragglers to the house for a sing song and my mother always seemed to be able to rustle up plates of sandwiches out of nothing. Parties could be every other weekend with the radiogram blaring out 'Who's sorry now,' 'Kiss me honey honey' or 'The Good Life.' Everybody had their own signature tune to sing and this was followed by my dad's chorus of "Oh my what a rotten song."

My dad sadly is no longer with us but my mum still lives in the Gorbals. We will all be celebrating her 90th birthday soon and there will definitely be a big sing-song that night on 16th May. My sisters and I think we have been quite lucky in our lives and are so fortunate to have so many memories. Stories and memories of the Gorbals and its people are never ending and we are so proud to have been a part of them.

Best wishes Marilyn Hamilton.

Colin Mackie

Entertainment, like many things "when I was an Oatlands buoy", was quite an involved community affair. Much loved street games like rounders, kick-the-can and hide an` seek were always favourites on the pastime menu (and yes, I can admit the odd game of Chap Door-Run Away). Indeed, an intense game of hide an` seek could sometimes include around 10 to 20 kids, and by the time the last "come oot, come oot" was heard, it was well past sun down. Many a time when I was the last one hiding, I took it personally that no one seemed in a hurry to find me, in fact sometimes the "seekers" made their way home without bothering to let me know.....all together now..."ahhhhhh!!!"

The streets of Oatlands were always full of activity with many a windae having someone keeping an eye out for the weans and what we were getting up to and neighbours shouting down for you to go to the shoaps and you would get some pennies for your efforts.

Playing in the back courts of Cramond Street (especially at night) had a feeling of being in a Roman coliseum with a 360 degree audience from the many "windaes" above, some houses even having poles reaching from the ledge flying their flags of the washing for that day, (long johns at half mast!!) The call of nature way back then, resulted in the downstairs journey and the big treasure chest key that gained you access to the landing toilet, often I peeked through the keyhole and said hello to my neighbours as they went up the sterrs, or screaming as the light bulb went out during a night time visit.

Many a local kid like myself relished the unique sound of the one tone trumpet and call of "any old rags!!" as the rag and bone man came into the street. The challenge of coming up with the traditional "auld claithes" rate of exchange was thrown into chaos by those of us who flew past our parents on the way down the close with anything we could grab from our wardrobes, and much to our ma and da`s dismay, the occasional "newer" items of their clothing. The magical brown suitcase was then opened and the ragman gave you the choice from his buffet of gifts including, bat n baw, a balloon, toy windmill and a fascinating wee plastic camera containing a negative that you could see when you held it up tae the light.

Benny Lynch

Glesga has given us famous people, their names too many to repeat.
But I will mention one called Benny Lynch, born in 17 Florence Street.

Born in the Gorbals area when the auld tenements were still standing.
Benny entered the Boxing game, with his daily training so demanding.

As a Flyweight oor Benny wiz brilliant, never ever letting the fans down.
Going down to Manchester, beating Jackie Brown fur the World crown.

Glasgow and Scotland sang his praise as a boxer, Benny was oor King.
Watching him with pride as he beat all his opponents in the boxing ring.

When oor Bennys career wiz sadly over he abdicated his boxing throne.
With his biggest fight outside of the ring as he faced demons of his own.

But Benny's boxing fans throughout this planet hold him with great pride.
His name lives on forever especially in the Gorbals in Glesga's soo-side.

So in Benny's memory, we all want a statue of him erected and unfurled.
'Cause Benny Lynch fae the Gorbals was Boxing champion of the Wurld.

St Enoch's Square

Leaving the sunny Gorbals, at Carlton Place with buildings oh so rare.
I crossed over the Suspension Bridge to go over to St Enoch's Square.

Glasgow's corporation buses terminated there as many of us do recall.
With Saint Enoch's Hotel and railway station, looking down over us all.

Always a buzz about the Square, with the sound of busy people's feet.
Years later I drank in the Old Eagle Inn, just a bit along Howard Street.

And the subway station built of red stone, standing there like a shrine.
Today it is an outside cafe, with lots of customers sitting doon to dine.

Winchers met at Timothy White's Chemist, it wiz a weekly appointment.
Unlike Dizzy Corner on Argyle St, with a bad name for a disappointment.

Looking ahead you had Buchanan St shops as far as yer eye cood see.
Window shoppin is aw we done, too expensive fur the likes o' you n me.

But what hiv they done to St Enoch Sq as I stand there so mesmerized
A new shoppin centre, subways moved, an the area aw pedestrianised.

Dixon's Blazes

Aberdeen has its Northern Lights, which is a magnificent sight.
But we had Dixon's Blazes in the soo-side, to light up oor night.

Every night people in the Gorbals tenements saw the fireworks.
The sky-line lit up wae the blast furnaces of "Govan-Ironworks."

Folk all working there flat out, in that foundry's sweltering heat.
Some poor people having an accident to their arms or their feet.

Fae every street off Caledonia Rd you would see sparks and fire.
As that wee pug train took the molten slag over to the Molls Mire.

Dixon's Blazes gave people work over the years, which wiz great.
Until sadly with a recession it closed its gates in the year of 1958.

But it got demolished, no more us soo-siders saw its nightly glow.
And with its destruction, into the soo side history book it would go.

Aberdeen's still got its Northern Lights, Aurora Borealis is its name.
But without Dixon's Blazes lighting up oor sky, it jist isn't the same.

Porridge

You either loved it or loathed it and that's the honest truth.
Loving each spoonful of it or wantin to spit it oot yer mooth.

My sister sprinkled sugar over it I thought she'd never halt.
While I was totally opposite as over it I would sprinkle salt.

I used to sit and watch my ma stirring oats into that big pot.
As soon as she poured it into my plate I ate the bloomin lot.

Winter mornings the porridge acted jist like central heating.
Weans that didny eat porridge had faces always greeting.

Summer months my ma bought other cereals from the shop.
Either cornflakes or those wans that went snap, crackle, pop.

Got to say I wiz honestly glad winter came back and nae fibs.
Cause ma would make the porridge that stuck fast to my ribs.

Ye can buy porridge in packets into the microwave it will go.
But it is not a patch on the stuff ma made all those years ago.

The Pawn Shop

In the tenements of old with oor people living on the edge.
The pawn shop was our saviour with your articles to pledge.

Nobody liked to be spotted going in, it did take a bit of nerve.
If you saw a neighbour, you'd give them the old body swerve.

The one I remember was John the Pawn on Braehead Street.
At the junction where Cally and Rutherglen Roads did meet.

Each Monday morning my da's suit was pledged so it seemed.
But come Friday morning my ma went back to get it redeemed.

Cash was tight and our mothers would give each other a haun.
Although as a last resort they really thanked God fur the pawn.

My generation remember the pawn though some say it's a fable.
But if it wizny for oor Uncle there would be no food on the table.

So now my wee poem is over I hope it put a smile upon yer face.
For to survive in those days gaun to the pawn wasn't a disgrace.

U.C.B.S.

Who can forget the UCBS building it was a pure architectural feat.
Standing there so magnificent in between Moffat and McNeil Street.

Inside was the bakery where people all worked by day and by night.
Preparing all the ovens to make sure the bread we got was so right.

The delivery vans loaded up, bread and pastries that were the tops.
Then the drivers headed off to deliver to all of Glesga's Co-op shops.

A thousand folk all worked in here, charge-hands or jist plain Misters.
Soo-siders all nicknamed it - Uncles, Cousins, Brothers, and Sisters.

The Shan was jist nearby, where we got the bread at a cut rate price.
With the tea-bread and pastries a day old but still tasting so very nice.

In the Shan you'd 5 women working there, there wiz always a queue.
And for the sixpence that your ma gave you, it fed us fur a day or two.

Remembering back to that UCBS building, my heart still fills with Zire.
What a shame it got demolished in 1981 after gettin gutted wae a fire.

Lewis's

Who of you remember Lewis's store, in Argyles Street so many years ago.
Being taken there by your mother and your weans cheeks were all aglow.

The size o Lewis's was awesome different staff to look after aw your cares.
And going up and down the escalators or as we called it the moving stairs.

Downstairs was the cafeteria, for a piece of cake or maybe fish and chips.
Prices were oh so very reasonable and the ice cream made ye lick yer lips.

Now best of all was the toy department, it had all our weans' eyes popping.
Our ma's never had much money back then so it was jist windae shopping.

Then when it was Christmas time, Lewis's windaes were aw a sight to see.
Full of Christmas trees with flashing lights, oh Lewis's wiz the place to be.

When I grew older and had started work every Friday I had money a plenty.
Visiting Lewis's music department downstairs and buying aw the top twenty.

Lewis's now has changed, with many shops all showing their different motto.
Yet it only seems like yesterday, I was a wean queuing up fur Santa's Grotto.

Late 50's/Early 60's

So many memoryies of my childhood days, amid my smiles and my tears.
Life it seemed so marvellous then, I was entering into my teenage years.

Each week I watched Bonanza Ben Cartwright's family on oor TV screen.
Sergeant Bilko made us laugh the crime show was Dixon of Dock Green.

Tenement clearance in the Gorbals started, but wasn't yet into full swing.
Elvis Presley had joined the US Army but to all of us he wiz still the King.

I used to like reading the Sunday Post the Broons family and oor Wullie.
Rangers were the top team in those days but the Celtic had Charlie Tully.

The summer months seemed to last fur ever, the sun shining every day.
Don't dare get tar on yer whitewashed sannies yer ma would always say.

The yo yo's were the playtoy of the day us weans tried to do loop the loop.
Until a piece of plastic became the new craze we all called it a hula hoop.

And now the late fifties and early sixties always stay with me in my dreams.
Oh why did they pull or tenements doon, and send us to housing schemes.

Pre-Online Newspaper Days

Do you remember before we got newspaper alerts on our phones and lap tops.
Ye took a dauner doon the street fur yer newspaper oot the newsagents shops.

The shopkeeper would aye greet you, wae a smile he had for aw us poor souls.
Then you walked away wae the Daily Record,oh and a couple of well fired rolls.

Ye see before we had all this modern technology, getting yer hourly news tweet.
We got the Record, to see if auld Pat Roller had spotted any crime on our street.

To get fitbaw results on a Saturday, the Pink Times or Green Citizen wiz the job.
Or the Weekly News for the adventures of Andrew Glen and his Collie Black Bob.

Sundays we had a great selection of newspapers, that we all bought without fail.
Sports fans went straight to the back page for the latest news in the Sunday Mail.

But my favourite was the Sunday Post, reading it in front of the auld open coal fire.
Reading aboot Oor Wullie or the Broons family, for me this was my weekly desire.

This is the way it was years ago afore we had all this www dot com internet caper.
When we still had pounds, shillings and old pennies to buy our daily newspaper.

Shawfield Stadium

Fun years ago was watchin Sunday night at the London Palladium.
But greyhound punters all headed for a bet at Shawfield Stadium.

They went on a Tuesday or Friday night wae money in their pocket.
Praying out very loudly their dog would run like a supersonic rocket.

Most punters lost cash as their greyhounds were slow out the stalls.
And didn't have their fare home so it wiz a walk back to the Gorbals.

Also years ago at Shawfield ye had a football team called Clyde FC.
But to the support who went to watch them they were the Bully Wee.

A great wee team they were but now they hiv changed their ground.
Hoping fur better days and praying fame and fortune cood be found.

Beside dugs and fitba you'd speedway racing and a hall fur a dance.
A guy winning money on Friday night's dugs had money for romance.

But greyhound punters are happy people their misery is only fleeting.
Cos if they lost on Tuesday they were sure to win at the next meeting

Cumberland Street

The toon had Argyle and Sauchiehall Street to buy yourself a treat.
But nothing could compare with all the shops in Cumberland Street.

You had Saint Francis' Chapel with the Paragon Cinema next door.
A flea ridden Picture Hoose aw the hard benches made yer bum sore.

Butchers, Bakers, Linen shops, cant really name a shop not there.
The Barber's where a bowl got stuck on mah heid as he cut my hair.

Passing by Lawmoor St Police Station, the Polis were all tough cops.
But never gave it a second glance as we looked in all of those shops.

A pub was on every corner fur a man to drink a pint and a wee dram.
Women were oot for the messages while pushin her wean in a pram.

I'll never forget all of those shops walking wae my ma and my granny.
As they tried to spot a bargain us soo siders were known to be canny.

These Gorbals shops were better than Sauchiehall St in my estimation.
Sadly they are a thing of the past jist like Cumberland St Railway Station.

The Shows

Who remembers years ago when we were young and life so serene
And every summer we went to the Shows jist over in Glasgow green.

The Wurlitzer spun roon so fast and the Ghost train made ye scream.
Weans were eatin toffee apples or candy floss to them it wiz a dream.

Pop music was in the air as people all gathered there in their throngs.
Some gangs would have a fight, Cumbie, Derry or the Calton Tongs.

Yer ma and granny would play Housey Housey hopin they would win.
Fortune telling by Madame Za Za but it cost a shilling for you to go in.

Stall owners shouting out come try yer luck and win a coconut or two.
But I never saw anyone win one they must have been stuck wae glue.

See this is the shows that I used to know when I wiz a soo side wean.
Dive bombers and the big dipper so fast but I'll never see them again.

Because I left old Glesga Toon about a life time ago as the story goes.
But in my mind I'll always be a soo side wean gaun over to the shows.

Rain's a Pain

We Glaswegians are happy folks we are not very prone to complaining.
Except for this month of July, see it just hasn't stopped blooming raining.

Some of us left for the Glasgow Fair, to go to sunny climes like El Spain.
Where ye sunbathe on the beach every day and never ever see the rain.

Us poor souls left here in Glesga are disgruntled, that is the honest truth.
While the sales of umbrellas, oilskins, wellies have shot through the roof.

See half a century ago when our generation and me wiz only jist a wean.
We expected the odd wet day or two but no a whole flamin month of rain.

This global warming wae polar ice caps melting makes us want to greet.
Because years ago in the month of July the tar melted under aw oor feet.

Dry weather is forecast the Met office said, but kin you trust whit they say.
Much more o the wet stuff, the Clyde will burst and Glesga will float away.

Next month in August we pray for sunshine, and nae mere clouds so dark.
Cos if it dizny we'll live in a submarine and get Noah tae build a new ark.

The Barras

The World- wide famous Barras, holds memories for us all so far or near.
Glaswegians go there in oor thousands, fur a bargain that izny too dear.

Rolls of lino could be bought dead cheap, or a carpet at jist under a fiver.
Our thanks go to the lady who founded it, her name was Maggie McIver.

A trip on a Sunday afternoon wae my pals and me, when we were weans.
Standing there watching Irish Paddy the strongman bursting oot of chains.

Never forget the Snake oil man, or the one armed man selling racing tips.
The man selling hot chestnuts but the sweetie barras made me lick my lips.

The salesmens patter was dead brilliant, talkin the hind legs aff a donkey.
Always exchanging your goods next week if you found them to be wonky.

There wiz always a carnival atmosphere there, oh the Barras wiz the place.
Weans getting photos taken wae the wee monkeys, smiles upon their face.

Paddys Market shut, has to be one of Glasgow city councils biggest crimes.
The Barras is another part of oor heritage and has to remain so for all times.

Wedding Scramble

I think of an event years ago and I explain it without any preamble.
As adults and weans alike, got ready for the Weddin day scramble.

Bride and Groom jist newly married looked oh so happy and sweet.
And covered in confetti they went intae the weddin car's back seat.

Then as the car's moved away, the groom's window down it wound.
And from his hand leaped a mixture of coins, to land on the ground

Then hell broke loose as the coins were thrown, oh what a scatter.
Men, women and weans dived in to the scramble, age didny matter.

Pushin and shoving with elbows used, to try and get a penny or two.
Somebody got a broken finger and some poor wee soul lost a shoe.

The lucky wans who'd grabbed a penny went to spend it in the shop.
The unlucky wans looked a mess, the wean wae nae shoe did a hop.

Yes getting married then having a family, it is all part of life's gamble.
But not as much as diving in head first at the Wedding day scramble.

Chapter 1

All of the money in the World could never, or ever would, compensate for that terrible feeling of abandonment, having to leave behind the "soo side" of Glasgow when our tenement building collapsed in 1960/1 and I, as a thirteen year old schoolboy, and my family, were shipped out to one of the new housing schemes on the outskirts of Glasgow.

Even today as I write this book and I am 68 years old now, I still feel "cheated on" in having to leave behind my Granny Hendry, all the neighbours, my pals who I played with in the back courts of our tenements, all the shops and shopkeepers that I grew up with, the buzz of walking along Rutherglen Rd and Cumberland St etc as people went about their daily task of getting their messages (shopping) while stopping to get the latest news/gossip so we could tell the neighbours in our street all that was happening. We had no mobile phones in those days or internet so we relied on word of mouth news and couldn't wait to pass it on whether in a neighbour's house having a cup of tea or doing a bit of "windae hingin" and speaking to the next door neighbours from your tenement window and they in turn told you of all the latest news.

I was brought up in number 40 Fauldhouse St in the "upmarket" area of the Gorbals called Oatlands. My street was almost at the boundary where Oatlands ended and the Gorbals began, so I had my feet in both camps so to speak.

My first memory goes back to when I was around four years old and playing in a pile of building sand outside our close-mouth entrance. My ma and da had paid a local builder called Mr Montgomery (Monty) to take out the old fireplace and build a new one, and a new surrounding tiled hearth. I remember what I was wearing that day, it was short trousers with a cross bib type of attached braces, and I was enjoying myself playing in this pile of sand, never realising that later in my life that I would become a bricklayer for 46 years and sand and cement would be a part of my everyday work life.

In my street there was the "Steamie" or to give it its proper name, the wash-house, where our mothers and grannies went with their weekly wash and sweated in the heat, washing the families clothes and then drying them, then when they were finished, they piled all the clothes into a pram and wheeled them back to their close and "bumped" the pram up the stairs until they reached their house door. There were no washing machines or microwave ovens back in those days and the work our ma's done was unbelievable, they all should have been given a medal.

So there was me playing in the pile of sand, the "Steamie" directly opposite our close and St Bonaventure's Junior Secondary School abutting onto the gable end of our tenement house, or as everyone called it "Big Bonnies". This was the school for Roman Catholics and not far away you had Wolseley/Logan St where you had Wolseley St Primary School where children of the Protestant faith attended, including a lot of my pals that I played with. All of my life I took a person as I found them, whatever religion or even non-religion, they were and it's the same today.

So there was I, just over four and a half years old and I got sent to nursery school at St Bonaventure's or "Wee Bonnie's" as we called it. I remember the teachers were very nice and you were rewarded with wee gold or silver stars on your book by the teacher if you answered the questions correctly. You were always spoken to by the teacher by your Christian name, but what a shock came later when you started your first year of proper schooling when you were addressed by your surname, although as I look back now, this was the teachers preparing us for the world outside and perhaps to toughen us up. I didn't like school all that much, as all I wanted to do was play football with my classmates at playtime, as Glasgow, as we all know, is a football mad city. One thing I did like in the classroom, and I'm sure you, or most of you will agree, was the wee one-third of a bottle of milk we got. I loved it, but the thing I hated was "the belt" from the teacher, aw it didn't half bloomin' hurt. Well they don't get away with it nowadays. Some of the teachers were sadists in my view, giving you the belt or "strap" for any or no reason at all and I'm sure most people will agree with me.

Now as a five year old boy my pals and me were always playing football in the street, we did this as soon as school was over, while the lassies were playing skipping ropes or playing "baws" against the wall, and while we were all playing our street games, we were all watched over by either our ma's or neighbours who were leaning out of their tenement windaes. Of course we had loads of other games we played at as weans, kick the can and rounders etc and all us weans were loved unconditionally by our parents and neighbours. Unfortunately there were a few "bad men" who would have preyed on weans, but if this ever did happen (only once in a blue moon), then the shout went up and the men folk would go in search of this "bad man" and give him such a "doing" he wouldn't be able to walk for months, and this was all thanks to the neighbours who would have spotted him from their window or maybe in the street and the alarm went out. Fortunately, I only had ever heard of one experience of this happening when I was a wean growing up in the soo side.

Then as weans, everyday for us was an adventure. Who remembers "dreeping aff dykes" or being dared to walk along the top of one of the many walls in our back courts, and of course you would never back down otherwise you would be called a "scardey cat." As I say, there was so much for us weans to play at, and not only in your own back court but you would walk for what seems miles to the back courts of other peoples tenements. We also did some "midgie raking" and as I got older, then some days you would walk with your pals in the search for a "lucky midden" where it had been rumoured that there were to be plenty of "luxies" found. I always remember walking up to the Govanhill area where it was said some people who lived there were toffs and threw away untold "fortunes" isn't it great what imagination us weans had. I remember finding a pack of playing cards one day and you'd think I had found a million pounds!!

Us weans walked everywhere, the same as everybody else really, and you only ever took a ride on a trolly bus or maybe the old shoogly tram when your ma would take you over to the toon to do some shopping for something special. We had rakes of shops all along Rutherglen Rd and Crown St but most of all on Cumberland St in the Gorbals, which had so many shops it was unbelievable. There was always a buzz walking along Cumberland St. It was always packed with people going for the messages. I used to go there with my ma and granny when I was a wean, but as I grew older then I would go there myself or with my pals. We would walk along Caledonia Rd then go down Silverfir St or Pine St to get to Oatlands Square that had a playground there with swings and a roundabout, but it was always packed with other weans, so you had to wait till some wean left before you had a shot on the swings and it was magic, we had no money but it was an adventure and we loved it. Then off to Moffat St and cutting through the pend, or as some people pronounced it the pen (which was a short cut between Moffat St and Sandyfaulds St leading to Cumberland St).

There was a bakery and a horses stable for Jacksons Coal Merchants in the pen and we used to always look to see if one of the horses was there, but most times it was out on coal delivery duty, although later Jacksons would buy lorries to deliver their coal. Then coming out of the pen the first thing you saw was St Francis' Church, a magnificent building and although I attended St Bonaventure's Church in Caledonia Rd, I would sometimes go to Mass in St Francis', it was truly beautiful inside with a magnificent altar. When I think back now, we had so many beautiful Churches and Chapels covering all the soo side (with the occasional Synagogue then later Mosques), but with the Gorbals and later Oatlands clearances, the vast majority were demolished. Between demolishing the Churches and tenements we lost so many fine buildings it was a crime. Lots of the buildings could have been refurbished, but the greedy factors who took the rent money never looked after or maintained our tenements, and let them slip into such a bad state that some were past saving.

Now getting back to my story of me growing up. I was attending Wee Bonnies and was taught by a few teachers, but the one teacher I will always remember was Mr Darcy, he was a very good man and would always be cracking jokes to us weans. I remember one day him asking all of us "Right, what is the meaning of the word 'abundance'" and somebody put their hand up and said "It means 'lots of Sir'" and he answered "No it doesn't, it means 'A cookie doing the cha cha.'" Yes, he sure was a character Mr Darcy or wee Jimmy Darcy as we called him behind his back. I'm sure that you, the reader, had your own favourite teacher in whatever school you went to and remember them with affection, although there would be many other teaches remembered for all the wrong reasons.

There was one particular teacher in Wee Bonnies called Miss Henrietta and what a terrible frump of a wee woman she was, and in all of my years in school there I never once saw her smile, it's like when you have a nice teacher then you look forward to your class, but with Miss Henrietta everybody would dread it, nothing you did was ever right and oh how it made the class lesson seem so much longer. Us weans couldn't wait til' the playtime bell rang and we would get away from the "Dragon" as we nicknamed her. As the playtime started we would all be eating our "play-piece" and nine times out of ten this was a "piece on jam" that your ma had made for you that morning, then as soon as that was eaten it was back to us boys playing football with a wee tennis ball (larger balls were banned in the playground area as they could smash the classroom windows) while the girls would be playing "beds" or hopscotch which I think is its proper name, or using skipping ropes.

I always remember in Wee Bonnies (and probably every other school in the soo side) when we were playing in the playground awaiting the nine o'clock bell for school to start, that as soon as the bell sounded a song went up " The bell the bell the b-e-l-l tell the teacher I'm no well, if you're late then close the gate, the bell the bell the b-e-l-l." It's funny how something's stick in your mind from schooldays. We would then all line up in single files and march off to our different classrooms. Our toilets were outside in the playground, the boys on one side and the girls on the other side, with a drinking well attached to their wall where you turned the wee handle and a fountain of water would shoot up and usually with a queue behind you shouting "hurry up, hurry up." One abiding memory I have of the school toilets was that because they were outside in the open, then on a really cold day in winter time the pipes would freeze over and we couldn't use them, this resulted in the Headmaster standing at the nine o'clock assembly and saying with a painful expression on his face," I'm sorry boys and girls, but there will be no school today because the toilet pipes are frozen over." I thought he was going to cry but when we realised there was to be no school that day we all let out a roar that would have dwarfed "the Hampden roar." Us boys would head off to play football in the streets and the lassies would go home and tell their ma "no school today," then they in turn would be out in the streets skipping or playing "beds" etc. I always remember it was a feeling of elation when the toilet pipes froze over.

Overall I didn't like school and hated to be hemmed in all day long in a classroom. I always wanted to be "free" and being a typical boy I wanted adventure and travel. Well later on in my life after I had left school and served my five year apprenticeship as a bricklayer, that's what I done and travelled halfway round the world building bricks in different countries after I left Glasgow in 1968 when I was twenty years old but that's another story.

A lot of my pals were of the Protestant faith and attended the nearby Wolseley St School. On that point, my own ma was of the Protestant faith and when she married my da converted to being a Catholic. Like lots of marriages in Glasgow they are "mixed" and I have never had any hang ups about that in all my life, although what made me laugh sometimes was if my school was going to Mass on a Holy Day of Obligation and we passed a Protestant school with the weans in the playground, then they would shout out at us " Catholic cats eat dead rats" and some of my school would shout back "Proddy dogs eat fried frogs" which when you think of it is daft, but that's the way it was. As I said before, it doesn't matter what religion you are or non-religion you are, in my book I treat everyone the same regardless, and I have been that way all of my life.

By this time I was about six years old and my da was always working in the building trade for a firm called Melville, Dundas and Whitson, or as they were better known, M.D.W. He always left our tenement house about five-thirty in the morning as he was first man on the job to start up the generators, and as he didn't drink alcohol he would never be late and had the keys to open up the site every morning. Now with da leaving early in the morning time it was my ma who would prepare and light up our coal fire every morning. My ma and my Granda Hendry showed me how to light the coal fire, which really was an art form of placing the little kindling sticks like a Red Indian tepee, but only loosely so the air could pass through. We would then put a few crumpled sheets of newspaper underneath, then a few wee lumps of coal scattered around (not too many at first until the fire lit) then lighting the fire and sometimes blowing on it, until it caught fire. You would then quickly hold a sheet of newspaper over the fire opening and as the fire "drew" from the air above via the chimney pot, you would hear a "whoosh" as the sheet of newspaper you were holding caught fire and was sucked up the lum. Some poor souls set their lums on fire and the fire-brigade had to be called out.

I clearly remember going down to empty the previous night's ashes from the fire (all wrapped up in a couple of sheets of old newspaper) one morning as my ma was making the porridge. I went down the stairs and went to the open midden in the back court, then standing beside one of the bins in the midden I dumped the ashes, but what a fright I got as this bloody great big rat the size of a cat jumped out of the bin, and I thought it was going to attack me. I ran up the stairs to our second floor landing, two at a time and was panting like mad. I ran that fast I think I beat the record set by Roger Bannister when he beat the four minute mile!! My ma said "Oh you were quick son" and after my breathing got back to normal I told my ma what had happened. Needless to say it taught me a lesson, and every time I dumped the ashes in the midden after that, I stood well back from the midden just in case.

On the point of the coal fire, how many of you remember the coalman when he delivered to your house? Our coalman was from Jackson's Coal Merchants and ma used to leave a bit of cardboard in our street window to let him know if we needed one bag or two. When we heard his voice shouting out "Cahole" then ma would shout down to him "Two bags up here on the second landing," then every door in the house was closed and the coal bunker lid opened. Up came the coalman who would dump the bags of coal into our bunker in the lobby and the bloomin' coal dust went everywhere. We left the outside door open and tried to "whoosh" all the dust out of the lobby, those poor coalmen carrying all those bags on their backs day in and day out, they were unsung heroes of the soo side. There was another guy who came round our streets with a cart and he would sell coal-briquettes but we only ever bought those once in a blue moon, when you think nowadays we have central heating or electric fires at the click of a switch, although nothing was better than sitting in your tenement house in front of the open fire toasting a slice of bread or maybe a few marshmallows. You would be sitting there with all of your family listening to the radio (before TV came on the scene) and watching all the "different faces" you could see in the coal fire while drinking a cup of tea. Then when you had finished drinking your tea maybe your granny would "read your cup" from the tea leaves left in the bottom of your cup, and tell you what your "fortune" was going to be. Yes, it was the tea pot back in those days before the tea-bags came on the scene.

Just about this time my ma and da bought a new thing called a TV set from Stirling Hunters shop in Crown St. Before this came on the scene a night out for people was a night out at the "pictures" where you saw the latest film. Anyway we had this object called a TV set, although it only had one channel which was BBC1, now with TV being in its infancy then, you might only have had one programme on in the morning time for an hour and then for the rest of the day the screen would show a "test card" so you could alter the brightness and contrast to get a good picture. Then about five o'clock at night if I remember correctly, the TV shows would start properly and I was always amazed that this little box could show all these different programmes and people. In fact, I remember my ma washing me in the sink one night when the news came on and because I could see him (the newsreader) I asked my ma "Can he see me ma?"

We had neighbours come up to our house as I think we were the only family to have a TV set in the area and ask could they look at it, they didn't want to watch a programme they just wanted to see what a TV set looked like. I remember as I got a bit older I was allowed to stay up a bit later at night and watch a few shows. My uncle, Wullie Glasgow, (who was my Granny Hendry's brother) lived directly above us and my "auntie", Jenny Tarbet, from across the landing, (she wasn't a blood relative but we called her auntie because she was a friend of my ma's and we were never allowed to call adults by their first name) came in on a Friday and Saturday night from seven o'clock onwards to watch shows like "Sergeant Bilko" and "Quatermass" etc and about every twenty minutes or so my ma would pass round a plate with sweeties on it, then a plate with wee slices of apples or oranges on it, but when it was nine o'clock I had to go to bed. When I think back now, those early days of TV when we only had BBC1, all of a sudden we got another channel called ITV, which actually showed commercial advertisements, oh man we thought we were so spoiled!! Nowadays we have television 24/7 and all the Sky and sport channels, but it really was so different back in those days.

My ma went every week on a Saturday morning to Stirling Hunter's shop in Crown St and paid the weekly hire of our TV set. In fact they had two shops in Crown St almost next to each other if you can remember, one shop was for the electrical side of things and the other was for prams, cycles etc. Ma would take me with her when she went to pay the HP (hire purchase) and we always got the 101 trolley bus to Crown St and just at the junction of Rutherglen Rd, where it turned into Crown St. The trolley buses were also known as "The Silent Death" because they got their power from electrical overhead wires and were almost silent as they travelled. Some children never heard them coming and were sadly killed as they ran out in front of them. Now sometimes the "overhead conductor arms" connected to the overhead power lines would come loose and fall down. This was because the overhead wires were at a very sharp turn. This meant that the trolley bus conductor would have to fetch the long pole from underneath the bus and push it up to the "fallen arms," and guide them back onto the overhead wires. This happened quite a few times and could cause a bit of a traffic jam.

Then my mother and me took a dauner along Crown St and look into all the shops as we passed by and then turn into Cumberland St, and again walk past all those shops. There really were so many and like all mothers, she would buy me a sweetie from one of the shops. Passing by the Paragon picture house, St Francis' Church and a short cut through the pen into Moffat St, up into Caley Rd and then almost home to Rutherglen Rd, where she would buy some meat for our Saturday evening meal from the butchers, which I think was called Cochrane's. Remember in those days we bought food, milk etc on a daily basis as we didn't have fridges or fridge freezers in those days. I can clearly remember people leaving their bottles of milk on their window sills overnight in the hope that it wouldn't turn sour, or maybe filling up the kitchen sink with cold water and leaving the milk bottle in there. I know that people of my generation will remember this well and know it's what we done, but when I tell my grandweans here in London they look at me in sheer astonishment.

When it was Christmas time back in those days, my ma would tell me to write out a list of what I would like Father Christmas to bring me, but always saying to me "You can't ask for too much as his sledge can only carry one or two presents for each boy and girl." Then when I had wrote my wee list I would put it on the coal fire and it would whoosh away up the lum to reach Father Christmas. My big sister Jeanette, who was four years older than me, didn't do this (maybe somebody had told her something!!) Anyway, I remember ma taking me over the toon to Lewis's store in Argyle St to see Father Christmas in his grotto. What a wonderful exciting place Lewis's was, especially at Christmas time with the windows all decorated with fairy lights and Christmas trees and reindeer's etc. It sure brought smiles to the faces of us weans. There was a great big queue for Santa's grotto but I suppose that all added to the excitement of meeting him. I remember telling Santa what I would like for Christmas when he asked me, then after I told him he dipped his hand into his big sack and handed me a present. I couldn't wait to get back to our house to open it up but ma said that I had to wait till Christmas day morning.

When Christmas day arrived I opened up that present, it was a John Bull printing outfit, with all the letters of the alphabet made of rubber. You could join all the words together in a wee stamping handle, then you dipped it into ink that came with the present, and pressed it onto the sheets of paper and envelopes also enclosed, and hey presto, you were a printer!! Mind you, what a mess all that ink made of your hands, it took me forever trying to wash it off and I'm sure I wasn't the only boy who got a John Bull printing outfit from Santa's grotto in Lewis's. My other present from my parents that year was a plastic cowboy gun and a plastic gunbelt, aw I thought I was Billy the Kid and most of my wee pals got cowboy guns too as we were all cowboy mad in those youthful days of ours. There was another boy who lived in our street and he was called Ian Davidson, and for some unknown reason he had asked for a Red Indian outfit with a feathered headdress, plastic tomahawk and bow and arrow, well that poor soul was chased through all the back courts and up and down stairs with all of us Wyatt Earp's "shooting him dead" a million times over. In fact he got shot that many times after the second day of wearing his Red Indian outfit he threw it away in the midden, I still laugh at that to this day.

We never expected to get many presents from Santa way back in those days as life was hard for our parents, an apple and/or orange in a stocking which we hung from our bed and just one present, or a shiny new penny was more than gratefully received, unlike today when I think our children/grandchildren can be spoiled with all the presents they receive, sometimes pushing their parents into big debt.

New Year's Eve, Hogmanay, was a magical time of the year. I remember my ma would scrub the house clean from top to bottom and everything was spotless to usher in the New Year. I was sent to bed as usual but was woken up about eleven o'clock that night and ma would dress me up in my good clothes ("don't you get them dirty noo") and my sister and me with our parents would be sitting in the house waiting on the bells to chime and the hoots from the boats/ships berthed on the River Clyde. Now as I said, my da never drank alcohol, not even at the New Year, but my ma would have a wee sherry although there was whisky, rum, wine and beer in abundance on the living room table for everyone when they came in, not forgetting the Dundee cake and shortbread etc (there was enough food to feed an army). Then there was the non alcoholic red-cordial wine and Bulmer's non alcoholic cider, which I would have a glass, pretending I was drinking "the hard stuff." It's great the way a wean's mind works.

Now we would all be sitting in our house waiting on the bells to chime in the New Year as in thousands of homes, not only in the soo side but all over Glasgow and Scotland, we would have the TV switched on and it was usually Andy Stewart resplendent in his kilt singing all the Scottish songs. Then as the hands of the clock neared midnight, the countdown on the TV, everybody was counting down then "Happy New Year" and everybody would go mad shaking hands and kissing and wishing each other all the best for the coming year. My family all wished each other a Happy New Year as the cake and shortbread and cordial wine was passed round. We left the front door open for anybody wishing to "first foot"us and slowly but surely our visitors would arrive but the TV ended at half past midnight as Andy Stewart and his friends in the TV studio bid us goodnight, that's the way it was with the TV back all those years ago. Yes our first footers had arrived and the "haufs" were going down a treat, then it was time for the singing to start, everybody would take their turn to sing although some declined. I would be sitting in amazement listening to the songs being sung while drinking my glass of non alcoholic cider. My uncle Hughie Hendry, my ma's brother sang his party piece which was "Ramona" and he was brilliant. My uncle Hughie was a "weans man" and I loved his company. I stood up and recited a poem I had learnt in school and got a big round of applause and although I was only seven years of age I was thinking to myself that I wish I was a man so I could have a drink of whisky, but there were no worries there because when I did become a man I made up for all my youthful wishing with great gusto.

New Year's dinner was our dinner of the year, and my ma like all other mothers in the soo side (and all over Glasgow) made a special dinner which was magic. The English may make a fuss over their Christmas day dinner but in Scotland it was the New Year dinner for us that held the special appeal. Plenty of first footers came to our house and there was plenty of drink left on the table and loads of food. My Granda and Granny Hendry who just lived round the corner from us came for dinner as did my uncle Wullie Glasgow, it was a rare old time in our house but then all of a sudden the celebrations seemed to be over and we went back to a normal life.

I'm sure everyone of my generation will remember the "back court singer", that man who would sing with all his heart in your back court, in the hope that a few pennies would be thrown from some kind person's window and/or maybe a "jeely piece" and he would always say thanks. Who knows what had happened to this man in his life and what had befallen him. My ma always threw a coin down to him and she said "Danny son you never know what lays around the corner for you in life, and if you can help somebody then you can be proud that you have done a good turn." Perhaps that man had a family of his own one time and maybe they had passed away, or some other tragedy had befallen him, as ma said "There but for the grace of God go I." It always surprised but pleased me that this great community spirit we shared in the soo side would always rally round if there was an emergency of any sorts, and although we might not have had much money but what we had we shared.

Do you remember the "ménage" that your ma was in when she paid maybe 2/-6d a week and paid into it for thirteen weeks and when it was her "turn" of the menage she would get £1.10/- , that was thirty shillings in the old money, it's nothing nowadays but back then your ma could buy loads of things for her weans. On the thirteenth week the money went to the person who ran/organised the menage by collecting the money every week from everyone who was in it, and sure wouldn't your ma buy you a sweetie or two when she got her money. It was the same when the gas man came to empty the gas meter, he would unlock the wee padlock, take the box with all the coins in it and empty it on the table in your living room/kitchen and as he sat there counting it he would work out what rebate you were due and give it back to your mother. Of course us weans would all be watching this and be hoping a penny or two would come our way so we could go to the shop and ask for the penny tray of sweeties. Of course there were some poor souls who had burst open their gas meter box to get the money in there because of desperation, but they would have to pay the money back, unless it was reported to the Polis that someone had broken into the house and had done it.

I mentioned previously my Granda and Granny Hendry who just lived round the corner from us in Wolseley St, actually came from the Highlands and came to Glasgow looking for work. Once there, he met my granny and they got married having my ma and my uncle Hughie as their children. My wee granny used to look after me when ma was working and I was forever in and out of her house. My other Grandparents, Granny and Granda Gill from Donegal lived over in the Dalmarnock area of Glasgow's east end and I'm afraid I didn't see as much of them as my Granny Hendry but I loved them just the same.

I was seven years old when a terrible tragedy happened. It was the school summer holidays and my granny and granda decided to go for a walk along to Cumberland St. We had just passed the Ritz picture house on Caledonia Rd and my granda and me were playing "football" with an empty box of matches that was laying on the pavement and we kicked this matchbox right up to the Southern Necropolis graveyard, then we crossed over Caley Rd to Sandyfaulds St until we reached Cumberland St. I remember it was a sunny day and all the awnings were pulled down over the shop windows to keep the heat off of the wares in the windows, especially the butchers with meat on display. Passing by Lawmoor St we were all looking in one of the shop windows when my granda collapsed in front of me. He fell backwards and fell with his head hitting the pavement. Soon the ambulance had arrived and took us all to the hospital but when we got there the ambulance driver told my granny that my granda had actually died in Cumberland St when he'd collapsed, he didn't want to tell her then in case granny took a bad turn herself, so that's why he waited until we were in the hospital. I really couldn't understand all that had happened as I was only seven years old, this was my first encounter with death and the memory of that day has stayed with me all of my life, it was so very sad. My granda was a good man.

Chapter 2

With the exception of my Granda Hendry dying in Cumberland St, I have so many happy memories of walking along it. The Paragon Picture House or as some people nicknamed it the "flea pit," was at the corner with Mathieson St and I remember going to see the "pictures" there on several occasions, but the hard bench seats didn't half make your backside sore. It actually started out originally as a Free Church then later became a Synagogue for the Jewish population that once was prevalent in the Gorbals but I believe later on that a high percentage of them moved out to the Giffnock area of Glasgow.

I also remember always looking at the air raid siren that was on top of the low level roof of Lawmoor Street Police Station and wondering what would it sound like if it went off, but I never did hear it, so that was a schoolboy wish of mine never to be realised.

I certainly do remember a Barber's shop on the right hand side of Cumberland St (looking towards Crown St) and my ma used to give me the money to get my hair cut there, he must have been really cheap because there were other Barbers shops nearer to Fauldhouse St where I lived. I do recall walking along to it and sitting on the chair awaiting my turn. When it was my turn the Barber would place a couple of wee planks of wood over the arm rests for me to sit on and then produced a bowl, I'm sure it was a metal bowl. He would plonk this on my head and cut away like a demon, although as a seven year old boy I wasn't interested what my hair looked like, but when I look back at one of my school photos of the time, it was definitely "a bowl haircut," not like a few years to come when all of us boys went to the Barbers and were asking for a "Tony Curtis" or Perry Como" haircut in the late 1950's early 60's.

At that age of my bowl haircut days, all I was interested in was playing football in the streets. One of my pals who went to Wee Bonnies school called Robert Fairchild, lived just up from Cumberland St on the corner of Gilmour St and Caledonia Rd and after getting my haircut I would see him in the street playing football and join him for a kick about before going back to my house.

Now talking about Gilmour St, it had a lovely smooth road and in the summer months if we were lucky enough to have been given a pair of roller skates, or if one of our pals had a pair of roller skates, we would "get a shot of them," and it was great zooming along the street. Even better still, one of us might have made up a "bogie," which was an old wooden crate which we refurbished with a plank of wood with the castors from a roller skate underneath and the crate standing on end (so someone could sit in there). Your pal would be the driver and you would be whooshing up and down the street thinking you were the "cats whiskers" and back in those days of the mid 1950's, there was hardly any cars in the streets, so there wasn't much chance of being knocked down, in fact, the only vehicles you saw were mostly work vans, oh yes that Gilmour St was a great street to skate on.

I remember one day, it was during the summer school holidays and we had been playing in Gilmour St just past the swing park there on Orchard St. As me an my wee pals were walking along there, this man and woman carrying a baby wrapped up in a shawl came over to me and held me a "Christening piece." I wondered what they were doing and when I opened up this piece of paper, inside it was two plain buttered digestive biscuits and in the middle of the biscuit was an old Florin coin (a 2/- coin). Well I ran all the way back to our tenement and showed it to my ma, who in turn told me it was an old Glasgow/Scottish custom that when a baby was being christened it was tradition to pass over a Christening piece for good luck to a child who was the opposite sex of the baby. So, if the baby, as was in this case a girl, then the first boy the parents seen after the baby was Christened was given the Christening piece and vice versa if the baby was a boy. My ma said I could keep the money as it was good luck so I ran down to see my pals and we went to "Irish Paddy's" shop. Irish Paddy's was just after the Coronation Bar Public House and I treated them all to the penny tray of sweeties then we all went back to Gilmour St to eat all our sweets. I spent the whole of the 2/- piece in the shop as the word had got around that Danny Gill was a millionaire (ha ha). I found out that day that I had made so many new pals it was unbelievable, the memory of being given that Christening piece has never left me but I was never given another one.

Us weans played everywhere but there was one place that always was a mystery to me, it was a kind of open park but the gate always had a padlock on it and us weans, being adventurous, always climbed over the railings and played in there. It was between Waterside St and the Coronation Bar (which stood at the start of Caledonia Rd). Actually it was open ground and very level and ideal for all us budding young footballers to play on. We played football there a good few times until one day this big policeman called us all over and told us we must not ever play football in their again. He told us that, very sadly, quite a few times over the years, weans just like us would be playing football and because the River Clyde was right beside it, if the ball went into the river, quite often weans would try and retrieve their ball and unfortunately would fall in and drown. This was why the gate was always padlocked, so we never played in there again.

On the point of the police, just along a wee bit from there was Hutchesontown bowling green and there stood a police box, they were all over the soo side these police boxes and always painted blue. They all had this wee flap on the door about three foot high from the ground, it was the emergency phone for the fire brigade, ambulance and police (remember back in those days hardly anybody had a phone in their house, mobile phones and the internet hadn't been invented). Well I suppose with us weans being dare-devils, we would open this wee flap on the police box and shout into it "There's been a murder" and run away. Of course we shouldn't have done this and we were told one day by a man passing by that he knew our da and was going to tell him unless we stopped doing it. I never done it again because that put the" frightners" on me and just the thought of my da finding out made my knees go bloomin weak.

I remember a wee pal of mine, Billy Harvie, he lived in the close between the Glue Pot Pub (at the corner of Braehead St and

Wolseley St) and Frank Baltoushla's newsagent shop. Billy was in the class below me at Wee Bonnies but we played football in the same side in the playground and one morning I will never forget was when John Docherty (Doc), who was also in our side, broke his leg. We could clearly hear the "crack" and we tried to lift Doc up but he was saying "No don't move me, my leg's broke, I know it is." Well that was Doc off to hospital and got a plaster, or as we called it a "stookie" on his leg. He was told to take things easy but eventually when he came back to school wearing his " stookie " all the class signed our names to it and being football mad like the rest of us, Doc pleaded to play with us at playtime so we put him in goal, now how was that for dedication.

Do you remember going to the Co-operative Shop? There were so many of the Co-op's shops covering all the soo side. From Fauldhouse St where I lived, if you walked for five minutes one way you would reach the Co-op shop in Polmadie Rd in Oatlands or walking the other way you would arrive at the Co-op shop at Snowden St/Rutherglen Rd in the Gorbals. My ma always used the shop in Rutherglen Rd and I think this is because when she married my da their first house was in Snowden St and she felt "at home there."

I clearly remember going to that Co-op shop with my ma and standing in amazement as the money my ma gave for her messages was put into a wee kind of cup and it was attached to overhead wires and the person who had served us then gave it a nudge and it would whizz on these overhead wires up to the cashier who was sitting at a till above everyone. The cashier then in turn would take the money and put the change and receipt back in this wee cup and it would whizz back down to the assistant to give to my ma. I always thought in my youthful eyes that this wee cup whizzing about was like something out of a space book comic and it reminded me of the space ships in "Flash Gordon" that we saw at the pictures on a Saturday.

Then who could ever forget your Co-op "divvy number?" It was the number your ma had, and every time you bought something you gave your ma's divvy number and at the end of the year she got her "dividend" money which had accumulated over the year with all the messages she had bought. One of the things in life that I will never forget was my ma's Co-op "divvy" (dividend) number which was 57824. It was embedded in my mind forever and "under no circumstances" was I ever to forget it. Later when I was older and I was going to get my ma's messages from the Co-op, the last thing she would say was "And don't foget my divvy number."

I mentioned earlier the newsagents shop ran by Frank Baltoushla and his wife Angela. His shop was right beside the Glue Pot Public House and it seems he had everything in there, newspapers, comics, sweeties, marbles (or jauries as we called them) cigarettes and countless numbers of everything else. If you were short of money, there was also a "tic book" which a lot of people relied on to get things until they had the money to pay. Like most of the shops all over the soo side, you could always get your messages on the tic until you had the money to pay back, between this and the pawn shop it kept many a family from starving. Frank's shop was always beautifully decorated at Christmas time in fact it was absolutely magic with wee flashing fairy lights and a Christmas tree. Us weans used to stand in amazement while looking at it. Later on in life when our tenement collapsed and we were moved out to South Nitshill, Frank actually bought a wee van and came round our housing scheme selling ice-cream, fags and bottles of ginger etc because all the new housing schemes hardly had any shops in them, unlike the tenement buildings that we had grown up in that had shops in every street.

My da's hobby was electrics and he had a tape recorder. He used to get all of the family to speak into a microphone and then we had the pleasure of listening to our own voices when he played the tape back, we felt like film stars. Da also loved taking photos with his 35 mm camera, it's just a pity now that all those old photos have been lost over the years, then with me living and working in different countries, my photos went missing too. Da as I said didn't drink or smoke and all his wages went into our house, in fact every Friday night in life my da came back home and held my ma his unopened wage packet, and that was some feat. Then my da bought a telephone for our tenement house, but in those days in the early to mid 1950's hardly anybody else had a telephone to phone us up, so what used to happen at least once a week was da would give me four old pennies and tell me to go to the public telephone box beside Hutchensontown bowling green at the bottom of our street (well just over the road in Rutherglen Rd). I would go into the phone box and put the four pennies into the slot, dial our number and on getting connected I would press the "A" button and my da was at the other end of the line and the first thing he always said was "Hello who is it? " (ha ha). I mean who else was it going to be phoning up?

That was back in the day when hardly anyone used a phone, not like today when everyone seems to have a Smart phone. I sometimes think that if our grandparents could come back and actually see a phone that fitted in your pocket and could take photos and also tell you when the next bus was due and tell you the weather forecast well they wouldn't believe it. I remember when at a later stage in my life when these new mobile phones came on the scene, I would wonder why in heavens name people would want to speak to each other while walking down the street with this thing stuck in their ear. Nowadays as I write this book the mobile phone has become more or less part and parcel of our daily lives so unlike when we used to have to use the phone in the street with the "A" and "B" button.

On the point of the street phone with the "A" and "B" button, if you actually lifted the receiver up and tapped a telephone number on the cradle where the phone rested then you would get connected (so I heard!!!). Sometimes the scallywags would shove a piece of newspaper up the "B" button chute, so if you dialled a number and there was no answer you pushed the "B" button and your four pennies came down. Now if this happened to an unsuspecting person then the four pennies wouldn't drop down, the person would walk away unhappily and the scallywags, who would see this happening, would go into the phone box, remove the bit of newspaper and hey presto the four pennies would land in the chute and off they would go with their loot.

Another treat for us back in the day was the "wedding day scramble." When the newlyweds would come out of Church they would sit in the back of the car and as the car was driving off, the window was wound down and the bridegroom took a handful of coins and threw them up in the air. Pandemonium was let loose as everyone was diving in head first to try and get to one of the coins that was lying on the street. There was weans and women all fighting each other, elbows being nudged into people's ribs, it was some sight to see. News had been going round for hours earlier that so and so was getting married and hours before the wedding took place the crowd had started to gather. I was one of them that took part in this ritual but all I ever got was just one penny but plenty of cut hands and bruised knees. This was one of the events that happened in the soo side that people of my generation will remember well and smile at.

Opposite the Glue Pot pub was a Sunday school building or the "Band of Hope" as us weans nicknamed it and "Auntie" Jenny Tarbet, our neighbour on our landing, was one of the organisers/teachers in there and some Sundays after attending Mass in St Bonaventure's Church we would be passing by it and if my "Auntie" Jenny saw me then she would say "Do you want to come in?" and I did. There would be a few hymns sung, then to our delight some cakes and buns appeared and a glass of ginger, it was great, until our Parish Priest Father Gilmartin heard about this, and after Mass was finished the following Sunday, he was ranting and raving about Catholic weans attending the Sunday School and how wrong it was. I mean to us weans it was free buns and ginger but he was going ballistic. To be truthful, most of us weans were intimidated by Father Gilmartin who was full of fire and brimstone, so much so that if I ever saw him coming towards me in the street then I would cross over to the other side and that I think says it all. There was another Priest from St Bonaventure's called Father

Cunningham and what a lovely kind man he was. I would always acknowledge him in the street if I ever saw him, whatever religion we are/were then in my book we should respect each other's.

Just beside the Sunday School in Braehead St was John McKintyre's Pawn Shop and I went there a good few times with my wee Granny Hendry, usually on a Monday morning and this pawn shop as with all the others throughout the Gorbals was a life saver to many mothers and their families. There was many an item pawned there on a Monday (da's suit) and the money received gave the family food on their table for the rest of the week, of course when the man of the house handed his wages to his wife she would redeem his suit, so he could wear it on Saturday night and be none the wiser for it. This was how hard it could be for some families in the soo side. How the mothers kept all their weans fed and clothed in those hard off times was wonderful, and they in turn should have all been given medals. Of course us weans at the time didn't realise all this but now as we look back it is with love and amazement how they ever coped, and there was no social security payments like there are today.

Now how many of us have memories of playing in the back courts of the old tenements, dreeping aff dykes, climbing up to the roof of the wee washhouse or lassies "playing shops" and everybody "paying" with pieces of broken plates and remember if your piece of broken plates or wallies as we called them had a patterned edge or showing a wee bit of "'gold'" on it then that piece was worth twice the value as that of an ordinary wally piece. So with all this playing about in the back courts, you tended to get hungry and then the famous shout went up to your ma's window, "Aw ma gonnae through me doon a jeely piece?" (It's funny how your own ma knew it was your voice and not another weans.) Then a few minutes later you ma would have a jeely piece ready for you, all wrapped up in the waxed bread paper that the loaf of bread came in. She threw it from her window and you always tried to catch it but never did, and it landed a few feet away with a splat on the ground which made it a "compressed" jeely piece, but how we loved it and even to this day I still have the odd jeely piece in my sheltered housing flat here in

London, evoking memories of our back court days. Sometimes your wee pals would ask you fir a bit of your piece and you always gave them a bit.

Playing in the back courts was our adventure zone and our imaginations as weans held no bounds. We could be playing Cowboys and Indians and when you were "in the saddle" of your imaginary horse chasing the Indians, you held the horses reins in one hand while slapping your backside with your other hand to make your horse go faster or if you had read a comic about Robin Hood then you were all his merry men and going after that bad Sheriff of Nottingham, but we never thought about rescuing Maid Marion because for us boys at that age it would be classed as being a sissy, and us rough tough soo side boys would never live that down. Of course years later would be a different story when it came to the fairer sex.

I always remember playing in the sunshine in the summer months and it really did get hot some days and I remember some of the pavements had tarmac on them but in the sun's heat it melted, and if you were wearing your new sannies or if they had been whitewashed then the tar was murder polis to try and get off and many a mother would clout their wean round the ear for getting tar on their footwear or clothes. I remember I used to like American baseball boots which were up a class from your ordinary sannies and you felt special if you were bought a pair. Then when we had the rain we all wore our wellies, there was nothing better than to go splashing in all the puddles that seemed to be everywhere, you would jump into a big puddle and splash all your pals and they did the same to you. When you went up to your house your ma nearly had a fit seeing you drenched from head to foot and sometimes the price to pay for that was you were kept in the house which of course you hated, this happened a few times to me and my pals would come up the stairs and knock on my door and say "Is Danny coming out to play Mrs Gill?" and she would say "No" while I was begging her, "Oh please ma, I'll no jump in any more puddles." Most of the time my ma relented but if I did come back up wet again, then I was put to bed early and that punishment made me think twice the next time.

Just a few minutes walk away from where I lived was the Ritz Picture House which was at the start of Caledonia Rd or Caley Rd as we called it. This is where we went on a Saturday either for the morning matinee or early afternoon show. I loved watching all the Laurel and Hardy films as they made us laugh, then we had the Cowboy films and Gangster films with George Raft etc. Now being typical weans, our mothers used to give us our picture money for getting in and a penny or two to buy sweeties, which was great and for whatever film that showed that day we played the part out in the streets when it was over. I remember watching 20,000 leagues under the sea by Jules Verne then all of us weans coming out and pretending to have a deep sea outfit on and wrestling with a giant octopus with an imaginary knife, ahh it was great what imagination we had as weans in the soo side.

Of course what we found out at the picture house was that if we got one of our pals to pay his admission money, go into the picture hall, then go to the toilets where the fire exit door was situated and open it, all us weans would stream in and in the darkness of the cinema try and get to a seat before the usherette could shine her torch on us. Of course, the usherette was going mad trying to catch us and shouting out "I know your mammy and I'll tell her." It was sheer pandemonium for a couple of minutes, we must have drove that poor Usherette mental every Saturday. Of course because we hadn't paid our admission money into the pictures we had all bought rakes of sweeties with it and this is what made Saturdays all the more special to us, although one Saturday as we burst in from the fire door exit, I got caught and was thrown out of the Ritz and I remember having to wait ages till the show was over to meet up with my pals again.

There were so many different picture halls to choose from in the Gorbals and as I got a wee bit older then my ma allowed me to go to the Bedford, the Coliseum, Greens Playhouse and the George etc and it really was magic, sitting there watching Pearl and Dean advertising all kinds of movies etc, then Pathe News, followed by what films were showing the following week. In those days of course we had an "A" film and the "B" film with an interlude so the ice cream girl could sell her wares to us, as she stood there with her tray strapped to her back, a Kia Ora orange drink or choc ice or maybe a packet of peanuts. You had to watch yourself when you went into the picture house at first because it was so dark (that's if you were late going in), the Usherette would shine her torch on an empty seat, otherwise you might trip over your feet because it was that dark.

You would sit down and watch your film. The "A" film could have been a Cowboy, Gangster or Love story etc and the "B" film could be not bad either, although it was a bit shorter than the "A" film, and there was many a time a Scotland Yard mystery narrated by Edward Lustgarten was shown as the B movie. The stalls was the cheapest place to sit with the balcony being a wee bit dearer, and of course this is where all the winching couples went to, especially the very back seats. Being a wean I wasn't interested in all that smoochy stuff but I sure did when I grew older, in fact in years to come I would go into the pictures and never even see the film, I think we've all been there folks.

I remember going to the George Cinema in Crown St and watching Charlie Chaplin in "The Great Dictator" with my big sister (remember I was only seven years old at this time) and I got my finger jammed in the seat when I folded it down and it was painful. I said to my sister Jeanette that I wanted to go home but she said no (as she was supposed to be looking after me and ma would give her a telling off), so my sister kept feeding me sweeties to numb the pain of my finger so that was good, however, the film "The Great Dictator" was boring, it was about Charlie Chaplin acting as a double for Adolf Hitler, and I thought because it was Charlie Chaplin that it was going to be a funny film. It's funny how some things stay with you all your life.

Overall the picture houses were a magic place to go for a night out although slowly but surely from about the early 1960's with the advent of TV they started to die a death as many people had TV sets in their houses and preferred to stay in and watch the box. Yes, Coronation St had started by this time and was the talk of the steamie. Lots of picture houses changed into bingo halls and with the chance of winning some money many a soo sider would go and try and get a full house, while sharing their winnings with their pals. Then later on, as we all know, the Gorbals clearance saw all the picture houses/bingo halls demolished for new housing.

It really did sadden me that some of the tenements were coming down, remember this was 1955 and I was only seven years old, but I couldn't imagine in my youthful eyes that years later the vast majority of the soo side, Laurieston, Gorbals, Hutchensontown and Oatlands would be more or less flattened, and although this would be bad enough, the loss of that close knit community spirit would also disappear. It's not that I'm against change. As I write my book today, the new buildings (after disasters like the Dampies, Queen Lizzie Square etc) are structurally fine, sound buildings and the people of the soo side today are brilliant, but it was the loss of our community spirit and stopping for a chat with the neighbours as we went for the messages in the shops of the tenement era that upsets me.

I remember as a wean another place of adventure we would go to was the Southern Necropolis Graveyard, just past the Ritz Picture House on Caley Rd. This was built because the original Gorbals graveyard, the Rose Garden, or "The Rosie" as it was nicknamed, which stands on Old Rutherglen Road opposite the Twomax Building was full. Now we climbed over the old railings and lowered ourselves into the graveyard and would be playing hide and seek amongst all the old gravestones, but never once harming or damaging the burial ground. Well you can imagine all the wild thoughts conjured up in our heads of stories we heard about Vampires and Dracula, and in our youthful imagination we would look at some of the headstones to see if a Vampire had ever been buried there, well we never found one!! There are a few famous people buried there (or their earthly remains I should say) and a few people that spring to my mind are Thomas Lipton, famous for his food stores, Alexander Thomson the renowned architect, Alan Pinkerton of the famous Pinkerton Detective Agency in the U.S.A. etc, but in those days when we were weans there was a famous statue to us called "The White Lady" erected in remembrance to John Smith his wife and their housekeeper but us weans never knew about that. I later found out though that John S Smith was a wealthy carpet manufacturer and he lived with his wife Magdalene in the posh area of Langside Avenue, Glasgow (which I believe is in the Battlefield area past Queens Park). John Smith's wife, Magdalene and their housekeeper, Mary McNaughton, were knocked down and killed by a tram in Queens Drive on a wet windy day crossing the road. This was because their umbrellas were up to shelter from the rain, and this is how they never saw the tram coming and the monument is a solemn and fitting memorial to this tragedy.

All us weans knew that if you passed by the White Lady statue then she would turn her head and you would turn to stone, so if you saw or thought you saw her turn her head, you had to run around the statue dead fast shouting out "White Lade, White Lade, White Lady" three times and you wouldn't turn to stone. I don't know how this came about but the statue put the fear of God into us weans, and every time we saw the statue we would comply with its ritual otherwise you would turn to stone and your ma would kill you!!

The Southern Necropolis is such a vast graveyard and boys and girls from the soo side over the years would, on a hot summer's day, go and sunbathe there maybe with a bottle of ginger and some food. It really has some wonderful readings inscribed on some of the headstones and today is looked after by a volunteer group who do so much for its maintenance, but back in the days when my pals and me were searching for Vampires this didn't occur to us as were out for a bit of adventure, although on one occasion a shout went up "I see a Vampire." Well there was pure panic as we all ran to the railings, trying to be first one over and get to safety but later on laughing about this false sighting of the Southern Necropolis Vampire.

Opposite, or maybe down a wee bit from the Southern Necropolis you had St Bonaventure's Church which actually started off life as the Buchananan Memorial Free Church then was reconsecrated as St Bonaventure's Church in 1953 as St Francis' Church in Cumberland St couldn't cope with all the people attending Mass there. Opposite St Bonaventure's you had a wee row of railway cottages that abutted the Southern Necropolis Graveyard at one end and abutted the Ritz Picture House at the other end. These wee cottage like houses were for families who had the men folk working along at the end of Caledonia Rd at the Gushet railway sidings. All these cottages had small gardens in front of them which was very rare for the Gorbals area. Right at the back of these cottages you had the Caledonia Garden allotments, where people could grow their own vegetables. The main entrance to these allotments was on Braehead St just at the Glue Pot Pub. I remember one day a year in the summertime, the allotments opened their door and they held a summer fete where the people who grew their vegetables had them on sale. I remember one of those days my Granny Hendry buying me a stick of rhubarb from one of the people (and they had a wee bowel of sugar on their stall so you could dip your rhubarb in it). Other stalls were selling potatoes or cabbages etc but the most visited stall by us weans was a stall selling glasses of ginger.

Later on these allotments were all bulldozed, plus the Ritz Picture House to make way for the Oatlands Regeneration, although Braehead St comes under the Gorbals area nowadays and not Oatlands. What I always said was, where Braehead St meets with Caledonia Rd, this was the end of Oatlands and the beginning of the Gorbals and vice versa. To me the Greater Gorbals area consists of Laurieston, Gorbals, Hutchensontown and Oatlands and what is Glasgow's famous soo side.

As I write my book today I must tell you a funny thing. A few years ago (2012) I was on holiday back in Glasgow and revisiting the soo side for the first time in almost 45 years. I had just got off my train at the Glasgow Central Station, checked into my hotel and was having a drink in the Laurieston Bar in Bridge St when I got talking to this guy and he said to me what is the name of the street that runs along the Southern Necropolis wall and I said "There is none," I said "You must be getting mixed up with Braehead St" and he said "No, there is definitely a street running down beside the wall of the graveyard." I couldn't work it out, so the following morning I went back to see Fauldhouse St, where I had been brought up, but before this I went to the Southern Necropolis. Low and behold the guy I had been speaking to in the pub was right and I was wrong as there now stood new houses and a street called Caledonia St, but when I had lived in the soo side there had been no street there as the railway cottages had occupied that place.

I have only learned to use a computer/lap top over five years ago when my eldest daughter paid for me as a birthday present to go to an Adult Education Learning Centre here in London where I now reside and I must say it has opened up my eyes to a world out there that I never knew existed. I looked at photos online of the soo side tenements that are still fresh in my mind, but I also looked at how the soo side looks nowadays and I couldn't believe it, in fact I still can't, but I will explain that all later on in my book as we go along. At this stage of my life I was only seven years old and still only a young boy but what an experience living in that era of the tenements and all that went with it.

Chapter 3

Now the year is 1956 and I'm eight years old and new neighbours move into the close next to us, they're a couple called Mr and Mrs Boucher. She was a Glasgow girl and Mr Boucher was Jamaican, and everybody called him Fitz as his first name was Fitzgerald but I always called him Mr Boucher, as my mother had brought me up to address my elders that way, unless they were good friends of our family and then, like lots of weans then, we called them "uncle" or "auntie." They had a daughter called Christina and she was a lovely chocolate brown colour and we became very good friends. Christina joined my school class in Wee Bonnies and I remember us weans in the sooo side had never saw a black person before and people were coming up to Christina and touching her "for good luck." I saw her as my friend and the colour of her skin never bothered me and that was how I would be all through my life to come, whatever religion or colour a person was, meant no difference to me as long as they were alright with me then I was alright with them. She was tall and slim and ran like a gazelle, in fact she won all the races when we had our school summer races over in Richmond Park. Later on in life when we had left the soo side to move out to South Nitshill, Christina and her ma and da moved into the house a couple of closes away in our street, but when I was twenty years old and started my travels I never saw her after that. I did ask her out on a date when I was about eighteen years old but she had a boyfriend so that was me shot down (as would happen a few times in my adult life), but it never stopped me from pursuing the fairer sex, with many heartaches to follow but I look back nowadays as I write my book and can smile, well there's no good crying is there (ha ha).

Actually Christina had moved into the same close as my Uncle Hughie, Aunty Annie and their children, my cousins in Fauldhouse St, and we were always playing together. However, a terrible tragedy happened. One of my cousins, Mary, who was a year older than me and my Uncle Hughie's eldest child, was standing in front of the open coal fire in her nightdress before going to bed and her nightdress caught fire and cousin Mary was very badly burned. She was rushed off to hospital my ma went up to see her and when I asked how she was, my ma would say "She's not too good son," then a few days later my cousin Mary died of her burns, and I could hardly take this in. We were always playing together in the streets or back court and being eight years old I just couldn't take in that I would never see Mary again. Even today, sixty years later, I always mention my cousin Mary in my morning prayers. What a very sad loss for my Uncle Hughie, Aunty Annie and my remaining cousins, and I still think back fondly of her to this day.

As I say, I'm eight years old and the year is 1956 and music has caught my ear and most of the other weans in the soo side. At school we were always singing the pop songs of the day, Bill Hayley and his Comets were singing "Rock around the clock", Doris Day with "Que Sera Sera", Johnnie Ray with "Singing in the rain" then a new singer came on the scene called Elvis Presley with Heartbreak Hotel and the music changed forever. We were all going crazy with "All shook up" etc which all followed and when we went to the local shop we would buy a penny bubble gum and with it you got a wee card with the photo of a film star or pop singer, and it was common for us all to do a swap with each other with these cards. Oh the music was great back then, and every now and then all over the back courts of the soo side the lassies would "perform a concert" standing on top of the midden roof and belting out all the hits and some of them were very good.

Then at school when you had the Christmas break up party or the break up at the summer holidays, you had all the budding pop singers belting out all songs of the day. I clearly remember one girl in our primary class called Geana Sweeney (McPike now) and at the Christmas do she stood up in front of our class and sang Elvis Presley's song "All shook up" and she was absolutely brilliant, and if I close my eyes now I can see her going through all the motions and she got the biggest cheer that day. I'm sure you, the reader, have many memories of the school break up party too. Only four years ago when I was visiting Glasgow I met up with Geana, we had contacted each other through Facebook and her and another person, Brian Donnelly, who was also in our primary school class met up in the Laurieston Bar in the Gorbals and had a tremendous day taking a trip down memory lane. Oh this internet business is terrific for contacting old friends who you never thought you would see again.

Back in those days of the tenements I'm sure you can all remember your ma taking her turn of washing the stairs, this would happen every three weeks as there were three families living on my landing and each dutifully took their turn. I remember my ma sweeping the stairs first of all to get rid of any dust and then with a bucket of hoat soapy water she would bend down on her knees and wash and scrub our stairs down to the half landing where the outside toilet was. Then, after washing the landing there she would go down the next flight of stairs to the neighbours below landing. I remember my ma always singing when she washed the stairs and they were spotless after she had finished. She used to kneel on this wee rubber pad to save her knees from getting rheumatism, then she would use pipe clay chalk to put a border either side of the stairs and it looked a million dollars when it was all finished.

No matter where you went in the soo side all the stairs were done the same, our mothers had so much pride in keeping our stairs all spick and span and would never miss their turn of washin' the stairs, even if they were sick. It was exactly the same with the tenement windows, they were always clean and shining and the net curtains were kept pristine clean too. How many times nowadays do you look at old photos of the tenements and the net curtains are pure white? Our ma's were very clean people back in those days, oh and you daren't go up a close if the stairs were being washed otherwise you would get a " Can you no see I'm washin' the stairs?"

On the point of the stairhead toilet, well unlike today when we all have inside toilets and baths and showers and heaters or central heating throughout our houses, the stair head lavvy or cludgie will go down in tenement history. Shared by all the families who lived on the landing (and you always went down to the stair head lavvy, never upstairs to it), so you could have up to twenty people all using it. All the families had a key for the toilet door and when you went in there it was so cold, and in those days the toilet roll was sheets of newspapers cut into squares and either hung on a piece of string or were pushed through a nail in the wall. You would be sitting there and you would hear someone coming down the stairs so you coughed to let them know the lavvy was occupied.

The cistern used to be high up and it had one of those long pull down chains to flush the toilet. There were holes and cracks in some of these lavvies and the wind would whistle through them, or worse still, you would spot a mouse or even a rat, and that did your nerves no good at all. Yes, health and safety today would have a field day. Then when you had finished you'd get back up the stairs as fast as possible and warm yourself in front of the fire after hanging the toilet key back on its nail in the lobby. Of course, sometimes the toilet could get blocked up and there was no good telling the factor (who you paid the rent to) as they only ever carried out work on the tenements once in a blue moon, so it was up to us and the neighbours to pour water down the pan until it was cleared.

Who can ever forget Paddy's market over at the Saltmarket, there was always a buzz about the place. Even though I was only eight years old my ma would take me there on a Saturday morning (and as I grew older I went to visit there with my pals). If my ma took me then we got on the 101 trolly bus going along Rutherglen Rd then turning into Crown St and over the Albert Bridge to Saltmarket and got off the bus just before Glasgow Cross and took a walk through Paddy's Market.

It was an Aladdin's Cave with almost every conceivable item you would need, whether it was an old tin bath, auld tackity boots, shoes with no laces, shirts, trousers, or even a fur coat. Not forgetting old tools, saws, trowels or maybe a lawn mower and piles of old clothes lying in big heaps on the ground, and the thing was, people were always buying these items and the buzz of all the crowd made it feel all the better. Oh you could have spent the whole day looking at all the stuff in Paddy's Market and with it being just over the River Clyde there was many people from the Gorbals used it and I remember my ma speaking to a few of the people she knew from the soo side.

There was a cafe on the other side of the road from Paddy's Market and it used to sell ribs and cabbage or plates of stewed beef. It was all basic down to earth food but it didn't half used to fill you up, but the tea was extra strong and stewed that it would have stripped the enamel off of your teeth. Then later on in life when I was a bit older me and my pals would walk all the way to Paddy's Market and have a good old look at everything on sale then take a walk over to the Peoples Palace on Glasgow Green and what an amazing building it really is. I always remember there were two jaw bones from a whale that formed the side of one of the doors, so after our day of adventure was over we would cross over Glasgow Green until we came to St Andrew's Suspension Bridge or the " Spenny " as we called it, and into McNeil St and walk back along Rutherglen Rd 'til we reached our houses and I'd be up the stairs and tell my ma I was starving. Like weans in those days we seemed to walk everywhere and it done us no harm at all.

On the subject of McNeil St, this was where I first went to the library and it was such a magnificent building (sadly today it's closed but the building is still in good conditioned and I hope in the future it can be re opened again). I remember the children's department was way up at the top of the building and it was here that I learned my love for reading. I remember my first book that I read it was a "Biggles" book. My school classmate Denis Smith who lived in Moffat St just round the corner had joined the library and encouraged me to do so too. So started my love for reading books and today I'm always popping into my local library here in south London or buying books from Amazon which I'm sure a lot of you readers do too.

As I said, my school class mate Dennis Smith lived in Moffat St at the bottom end close next to Ballater St and almost opposite that fine building was St Mungo Halls. I used to go up to Dennis' house and he had an electric train set which we would play with for hours or go over the street to play football in Hayfield St Primary School, this was after school had finished and we would go in there and play football with a wee tennis ball. We would play in the area with seats along one side of the wall (this was where the weans sat when it was raining at playtime as it had a roof over it) and this open/enclosed area made a great "football pitch " for us and many a game we held there until the janitor was ready to close the school gates, and he would shout "Right boys lets have you, it's time up." I think that the janitors in all the schools in the soo side were pretty fair (except for the odd one or two) and they always allowed weans to play in the school yards when school was over providing they were only playing and not up to mischief.

Just at the top of Moffat St where my pal Dennis lived (remember this was the bottom end of Moffat St which ran from Rutherglen Rd to Adelphi St, the other end ran from Rutherglen Rd to Caledonia Rd) well just round the corner stood a famous fish and chip shop called "Greasy Peters" and the queue outside of his shop, especially on a Friday night seemed a mile long. He really did sell great fish and chips.

Some nights when my pals and me had finished a swimming session in the Gorbals swimming baths, we would walk to Greasy Peters and buy a penny worth of scrapings, or was it threepence worth? It was magic. You had old bits of fish, and a few other left overs and he would pile them into your "poke" as we called it. In those days all your fish and chips or just chips were wrapped up in newspaper. My ma used to send me to Greasy Peters on a Friday night, although we had a fish and chip shop nearer to us his name was that good we used him. Anyway, after queuing up for what seemed ages, it was my turn and I would tell him what ma had told me to get, then when I got it with plenty of salt and vinegar I would shove it up my jumper and run quickly along Rutherglen Rd so it wouldn't get cold, while all the time breathing in all the salt and vinegar fumes, oh it was mouthwatering.

I would get home with the fish and chips and my ma had a couple of plates on top of pots and pans with boiling water in them and their steam kept the plates warm so we wouldn't have cold plates and we sat down and eat our meal. There had been plenty of salt and vinegar put on them and now was the turn for the broon sauce, we always used HP sauce and how we all enjoyed it.

Now next door to Greasy Peters was a shop called "Dirty Maggies" and she sold comics or you could sometimes do a swap with her if you had a real good comic (maybe a DEL, an American comic). She was a funny old woman with cut down gloves and her shop was always packed with weans, there were comics piled up to the ceiling in her shop. I always wonder where did the like of Greasy Peter and Dirty Maggie go when the Gorbals clearance demolished their tenement?

I know that people all over the soo side had their own favourite fish and chip shops like Anne's Fry or Mario's only to name a few but Greasy Peters was the one not nearest to me but close enough. When I try some of the fish and chip shops here in London where I live it just isn't the same and I honestly yearn for our soo side chip shops, but as they say, time marches on. I know today we can order Indian curries or a Chinese take away over the phone but they are not a patch of our fish and chips back then in the days when the tenements were standing. In fact as I write this I'm slavering at the mouth lol

As I mentioned earlier, going to the Gorbals swimming baths was terrific, it was here that I learned to swim just like thousands of other weans from all over the soo side. In fact, I always remember when I was eight and couldn't swim at the time I was walking along the edge of the pool when this other boy ran past me and bumped into me sending me into the water.

This was at the halfway point of the pool so it wasn't like the shallow end where I could have stood up, in fact I was drowning and trying to shout help but was gulping in water instead. As luck would have it, the attendant had seen what had happened and dived into the water and pushed me onto the walking area. I was fighting for breath but gradually calmed down, the attendant said "Are you okay?" and I said "Yes," so he said "Right get back in the water now otherwise you might be frightened to do so in the future." I did and went back to the shallow end but made myself a promise that I would learn to swim and within a few months I did, it's only confidence really when you think about it but I didn't half get a fright that day. I always took my own swimming trunks with me that ma had bought me and just paid the admission money into the baths. Some boys didn't have their own swimming trunks and that meant they had to hire a pair that belonged to the baths. They were skimpy things and had to be tied at the sides with a cord but a lot of the times when you dived or jumped into the water they came undone.

There was a hot shower where you went first of all before you went into the swimming hall, then you would run into the swimming hall area with your pals and as you entered the noise was deafening from all the other weans in there and a King's ransom wouldn't have made you any happier as you felt on top of the world. We would stay for as long as we could, then when your allotted time was up the attendant would open your stall door and drape your towel over the half door and if you didn't come out of the pool straight away he would blew on his whistle and say "Right, if you don't come out your towel is being thrown into the swimming pool." Well that was it, you couldn't argue with that, and we all jumped out of the pool and dried ourselves off. Oh what a magic time we had that day or evening.

Then on leaving the swimming baths, providing we had the money, we would take a short walk to Cleland St and go under the railway bridge to the hot peanut man. (I think Mr Chessman was his name). Oh the aroma of the peanuts and homemade tablet was so enticing and we would chip our money in together and buy some, eating it while walking home. I remember looking down Hospital St as we left the hot peanut man and thinking what a wonderful smooth road, it must have been ideal to use your roller skates on, much like Gilmour St where I had used roller skates myself, never thinking that in ten years time when I was a young man Hospital St with the

Clelland Bar would be a place I would frequent every weekend but that was in the future to come.

We would then cut through to Crown St and Rutherglen Rd, the way the 101 trolly bus went but with no bus fare on us we were happy enough to walk. This would take us past Florence St, where Benny Lynch the World Champion Boxer was born and bred, then if it was during the day we would go into the Gorbals Burial Ground or as we called it "the Rosie" and play for a while. Right opposite was an iconic building called Twomax where women sweated over the years in this knitwear factory it employed so many over the years and my big sister Jeanette had her first job as a sewing machinist among hundreds of other women and girls. Twomax's name I always just accepted and it wasn't till later on, in fact years later that I found out why it was called Twomax. In between the war years two men called Mr McClure and Mr McIntosh bought and took over the existing factory and made it into a knitwear factory and they named after themselves " the two Macs" or as we know it " Twomax".

Then continuing our walk home from Gorbals swimming baths we would pass all the tenement buildings that stood either side of Rutherglen Rd which would later on in years to come be known as Old Rutherglen Rd. Anyway, once we past Hayfield Primary School, Greasy Peters , Dirty Maggie's, McNeil St library, the Co-op shop and the Coronation Bar etc, never imagining in our youthfulness that all these buildings would be demolished with the exception of McNeil St library (now derelict), these were the tenements that we took for granted. I always thought that these buildings would be there, but the Glasgow City and Town planners had different ideas and it has always amazed me and saddened me that so many beautiful buildings were demolished when so many have could have been saved and refurbished. Just in that area alone you also had St Mungo's Halls and the United Co-operative Building Society building (which was fire damaged but could have been refurbished). Just look and think back to all those magnificent Churches, Chapels and Synagogues that used to cover the greater Gorbals area, and yes, lots of the tenements also that could have been refurbished but I'm afraid it wasn't to be and I do feel really angry about it.

Look at nearby Govanhill and the many many tenements still standing there and it makes you ask why?

On a cheerier note, my ma and da always took my sister and me away for our summer holidays just like thousands of other soo siders and one of my favourite places we went to was Saltcoats on the Ayrshire coast. Like most people we went away at the Glasgow Fair Fortnight when most people had the two weeks off from work. I remember the buzz in the air as we went over the toon to St Enoch's Railway Station (others went to the Central Station) for their destinations and I remember the two railway stations being absolutely choc- a-bloc, people were lugging suitcases about with a belt strapped round it in case it burst open.

In those far off days the suitcases with the wheels on it to pull around with you and making life so much easier hadn't been invented, and many a railway porter earned a few shillings carrying people's luggage for them. I remember all the railway carriages being full and everybody chattering away, oh it was so exciting. Then when we pulled into Saltcoats Railway Station and I felt like shouting out "yipee." Ma and da had rented a big room with two double beds and it was only a short walk from the station. I couldn't wait to go and explore the "new territory." Well there were cafes, restaurants, fish and chip shops everywhere and plenty of shops, although the best was the seaside where we went every day (providing it wasn't raining) and da would struggle with getting the deck-chairs assembled but somebody always lent a hand if you got stuck.

Sitting there enjoying the sunshine or making castles in the sand, it was like a different world altogether from the soo side. There would be people swimming in the sea or grandas paddling in the water and ma would always say "Splash some sea water on your face as it helps to give you a sun tan." Then you had the "shows" there and they were always packed with people enjoying the Fair Fortnight and you always met somebody from back hame and oor Granny Hendry came down for a day to join us, but she ended up staying for a few days. Even if it rained it didn't make you down hearted as there were plenty of indoor arcades to while away the time and at night time going for long strolls along the sea front while eating a poke of chips, this felt like heaven, not forgetting during the day you had an ice cream pokey hat.

We met up with friends who lived only a street away from us back in the soo side, and ma and them would have a good old natter but then soon our holiday was coming to an end and we were packing the suitcase to go back to Glasgow, but what a wonderful time we all had and we would always bring back sticks of rock or wee wally dugs to take back as presents to friends. Before we knew it we would be pulling into St Enoch's, or was it the Central Station? I can't remember which one now and we would then get the bus back to Fauldhouse St and as much as it was nice to go away on holiday, it was great to get back to the soo side and all my pals and neighbours and telling them all about it.

Later on in life ma and da would take us to Millport and the Isle of Man a few times, but nothing could beat going to Saltcoats for the Fair Fortnight as there was something magical about it all. Later on from about the mid 1960's onwards there was a new thing called a package holiday to Spain and instead of soo siders going to the sea side it was for many a holiday trip to the Costa Del Sol.

Oh yes, sun, sea, sand, sangria and pesetas. This was what enticed people from the soo side to go to Spain, where you could laze in the guaranteed everyday sunshine and go to the bars at night time and drink to the early hours of the morning while having a ball. The drink was cheap and you done the soo side shuffle wearing a big sombrero without a care in the world, oh yes, definitely Viva Espana.

On the subject of sand, well we had the "sony pon" in Richmond Park which was an oasis in the desert for us Gorbals and Oatlands people, and for some of the people from the soo side who never went away for the Fair Fortnight they could always have a day out there. It was such a big park with something for everyone. Oatlands people more or less just walked over Rutherglen Rd and they were there while folks from the Gorbals had a wee bit of a walk although they could always catch the 101 trolly bus from the Crown St end of Rutherglen Rd and be there in a five minute journey. There was the sand pit or "sony pon" as we called it where young weans could sit and play in the sand under the watchful eyes of their mother who would sometimes bring a blanket to spread on the grass and hold a wee picnic which might have consisted of a few hard boiled eggs, jeely pieces and a bottle of ginger and it made your day out all the better.

Older weans, especially the boys could have a game of football on the large grass area here beside the "sony pon." I remember this was the only place in Richmond Park where you were allowed to play football without the "Parkie" blowing his whistle and chasing you. I don't know why the Parkie chased us because we were dead fast at running and would leave him panting for breath.

Then further along in Richmond Park you had the rockery and flower gardens which were looked after lovingly, and there were always beautiful floral displays. This was a large area and there was always plenty of bench seats for us to sit on, the grass was always neatly cut and there seemed to be "keep of the grass" signs everywhere you went. Of course one of the best places in the "Richy" as we called it, was the swing park, and us weans would have a go at climbing the monkey bars, or rather swinging from one bar to the next, although usually your arms got tired half way along and you dropped down to the ground. So then it was off to the swings, sitting on the wee wooden seat and trying to "work yourself up" to a great height while shouting at your pals "Hey look at me." Then off to the big chute and who remembers bringing a bit of grease proof paper with you (the wrapper from a loaf of bread) and placing it on the slide, sitting on it and hoping the grease proof paper would help you slide faster!!

Now after the swings we would all walk over to the "ducksie " which was the pond of water that had beautiful white swans swimming in it. They were beautiful birds and had a very wide wing span, the old story was one of these swans could break your back if you angered them, but I think that was an old wives tale but I never put it to the test just in case! There was a model boat house there where men kept their model boats and at the weekends have them out in the water and they were great to watch. Later there was these "pedalo" boats that you could hire, you sat in them and worked the pedals with your feet and hey presto, you were sailing in the middle of the "ducksie." Just beside the boathouse you had a giant chess/draughts board painted onto a tarmac section and elderly men who I thought were ancient (but the truth is they would only be about 60 years old) but now as I write my book I'm 68 years old myself and don't feel "ancient" (ha ha). Ye,s the men would sit there with big long poles to move the chess men or draught pieces from square to square without having to leave their seat.

Some of us weans would go to the ducksie with a fishing net, (this could be bought from a wee shop on Rutherglen Rd opposite the park) and an empty jam jar and would try and catch some "Baggy Minnows." If we did, we put them in to the jar and would take them home to show to your ma and da, but you only ever kept them for a day and then got fed up with them, it was just the excitement of catching them that made us feel dead good. Now you had this stream of water called "Jenny's Burn" running through the park and flowing into the River Clyde but the smell from it was terrible. There was a chemical factory called Whites if I remember correctly, this was situated opposite Shawfield Stadium and they dumped their chemical waste into Jenny's Burn and this is what made it stink to high heaven. If I close my eyes, then I can still smell it, it was revolting.

It was here in Richy Park that some schools held their summer school races and I went over there with my school, Wee Bonnies. There was the sack race and the three legged race etc. Actually I came in runner up in the egg and spoon race and who beat me, it was my class mate Christina Boucher who I have talked about earlier, she ran like a gazelle and won most of the track races, it really could be a great day out for everyone. There was also a wee putting green there where for 3d old money, you could play a round of holes and think you were Jack Nicklaus. There were a few water fountains in the park in case you were thirsty, they had this big metal cup with a chain connected to it and you drank from that. Altogether you could spend a great day doing different things in Richmond Park and of course a wee bit of sun bathing in the summer months, then, when it was time to go home, everybody would walk along Rutherglen Rd till they came to "the devils tree." The devil's tree was such a horrible looking tree with big bumps and gnarls on it. Well the story behind the devil's tree was that if you didn't spit on it as you passed by, then you would get bad luck for ever, so needless to say most people spat on it as they walked past.

Going past Richmond Park for a few miles you would come to the wee town of Rutherglen and that could be another wee day out for us soo side weans. You had a red bus (SMT) and it left Clyde Street and went to Cambuslang, but passing Rutherglen on its way there. The strange thing about the red buses was you could get on them at the Clyde St terminus but you couldn't get off of them until you had passed the Glasgow City Boundary, so if you wanted to get off at say McNeil St then you weren't allowed to, you had to wait 'til you got to Shawfield Stadium, which is where Glasgow ends and the Burgh of Rutherglen begins. Sounds strange, but that's the way it was back then. Us weans would walk to Rutherglen and they had two picture houses, the Rio and the Odeon, so we had a choice of films to see. Our ma's would have given us the bus fare to Rutherglen and back, but being typical weans we walked it and the bus fare was spent on sweeties. I think most of us weans did that at some time or other (shhhh).

Just last year when I visited Glasgow for my now yearly holiday, I actually went out to Rutherglen to pay a visit and it's more or less the way it was when my pals and me used to go to the Rio and Odeon. The Rio has been bulldozed but the Odeon was still there, but had changed into a bingo hall but now closed. Main Street was more or less untouched and it felt like I was back in a time warp, all the wee shops were still there and I went into a wee tea room and told the girl behind the till that I had walked along Main St almost sixty years ago as a wean, I think she thought I was Methuselah. I had a few beers in the bars that had been there when I had grown into being a young man and went to Rutherglen when I was nineteen or twenty years old.

Chapter 4

I'm now nine years old and like most of the boys/girls in the soo side we either support Celtic or Rangers, and there's no disrespect meant to the other good folk who support other Glasgow football teams, like Third Lanark, Clyde, Partick Thistle or Queens Park. There's the green half of Glasgow and the blue half of Glasgow and that's just the way it is and that will never change. Now as I say, I'm nine years old and my parents won't let me go to Parkhead to watch Celtic play as I'm too young and I'm sure it was the same for other young lads who supported Rangers and wanted to watch their team play at Ibrox Park.

Just past Richmond Park you had Shawfield Stadium, which at that time was the home ground to Clyde Football Club, and a great wee football team they were too. Their fans nicknamed them "The BullyWee," Now I was allowed to go and watch Clyde play their home matches so off I would go on a Saturday and ask one of the men paying their money at the turnstile to give me "a lift over." At this time at football matches a man could give his son a "lift" over the turnstile without paying for him. So my pals and me would stand outside the gate entrance and say "Gonnae give us a lift over mister please?" Most of the men would lift you over, but you had quite a few who said "I have a sore back son." I personally made myself a pledge that when I became a man then I would always give a young lad a lift over and not be miserable like some of the men I had asked!!

Well, once inside the stadium I would take myself down to the perimeter wall surrounding the playing pitch so I could have a good view of the match once it had started. I liked watching Clyde play, but my love was for Celtic, just the same as the lads whose love was for Rangers. At half time in those days you had a big board giving you letters of the alphabet A, B and C and so on, this was actually the scores of all the other Scottish clubs playing that day, but you had to buy the match programme which gave you the "key" so A might have 2 -1 against it and when you looked at the programme it said A was Dundee v Falkirk, so at halftime Dundee would be beating Falkirk 2-1 and so on.

I would always ask one of the men who had bought a programme what was the half time score with Celtic and hope that they were winning. In those days at half time at Shawfield Park you had a photographer from the "Evening Times" newspaper walk round the park with a big flashlight camera and he would take a photo of us young lads standing there on the terracing. When the newspaper was printed that night (or was it Monday night?) then it would show you the photo of say us and one of us would have a white ring drawn around our face, if you were the lucky one then your da or ma would go up to the Evening Times office over Glasgow city centre and with proof via a photo, or taking you there personally, you were given the ten shillings or whatever for being the lucky winner. I never had the ring drawn round my head but my pal Billy Harvie did, lucky lad.

Shawfield Stadium was also famous for holding greyhound racing there on Tuesday and Friday nights and there was always a good crowd that turned up there. There were more losers than winners I'm afraid to say with the punters, although lots of people in the soo side would put on a bet with the street bookie rather than go to Shawfield. It also had a lounge bar and you could have a dance there too at the weekend. Then later there was motor bike speedway racing there, so Shawfield Stadium has always been a busy wee place. Sadly Clyde Football Club moved away from Shawfield Stadium to the Cumbernauld area outside of Glasgow.

Just over from Shawfield you had the terminus for the 101 trolly bus and my pals an me sometimes walked down there to try and catch a lift off the platform of the bus as it drove away or "cadging a hudgie" as it was called in Glasgow slang. The conductor of the bus knew what you were up to and you might just have grabbed the pole on the middle of the platform, but he would make a dive for you and you would have to let go, but it was all fun for us weans, although on a more serious note, a few children were knocked down and killed in the streets because the weans (God Bless them) hadn't heard the trolly coming, in fact they were nicknamed "the silent death."

You had all these beautiful red sandstone buildings in that part of Oatlands and they looked fantastic, but later on they would be demolished too. Some were refurbished but just like the Gorbals, they were all flattened for the Oatlands regeneration plan, it was such a shame. I remember walking along Toryglen St (where the singer and Glasgow showman Glen Daly lived) one day trying to get into Roseberry Park Juniors Football Ground to watch them train. They were also a good wee team, all juniors of course. In fact, their claim to fame was in the 1960's when the Brazilian football team were in Scotland for World cup matches they used Roseberry Park as their training ground.

Next to Toryglen St you had Polmadie Rd and up there you had the steam locomotive engine sheds, where the locomotives berthed and were checked out then fired up, ready to haul either carriages or freight to destinations all over Scotland and England. You also had rail sidings there where freight cars were parked up with coal in them and quite a lot of people in the soo side tenements got their coal supply from shall we say "falling off the back of a lorry."

Farther on a bit past the engine sheds you had the Glasgow Cleansing Department buildings where rubbish was burnt in the incinerator and the "clenny" vans/lorries parked up overnight. Of course the Malls Mire wasteland was past that again and this is where loads of molten slag was dumped by wee Puggy trains form Dixon's Blazes Ironwork Foundry which used to light up the sky all over the soo side at night time although it closed in 1958. There was a public house named the Molls Mire and it was situated at the corner of Polmadie Rd and Wolseley St but obviously is no longer there as it was flattened along with all the tenements. Going along Wolseley St leaving the Molls Mire Pub behind you came to Logan St and it was there you had the Logan Bar Public House, a few shops and a Bookmakers called Patsy Fagan's. Now my uncle, Wullie Glasgow, was a bookies runner (collecting people's bets as he stood in the close mouth of Fauldhouse St where I lived, because going into a bookmakers was illegal back then in those days). In fact the police used to raid this bookmakers shop and anyone standing in there was carted out to the waiting Black Mariah or Paddy wagon as it was sometimes called and taken to the police station in Lawmoor St or maybe Craigie St. The people were all fined for being in the bookies shop but Patsy Fagan always paid the fines for them. It seems so crazy but back then that's what happened. Thank God the bookie's shops were made legal in the early 1960's and nowadays as I write my book if you go into a bookmakers shop you have coloured televisons on the walls showing you all the different races and you can have a cup of tea or coffee and a sandwich.

My uncle Wullie Glasgow as I said before was a very kindly man and in his tenement house directly above us he never had electricity. What he had was a gas mantle to light up his house, having no cooker, he boiled the kettle for a cup of tea on a fire range encompassing his coal fire. My Granny Hendry (his sister) used to do the cleaning for him in his house and used to bring him a meal up every now and then although I think my Uncle Wullie used to eat out a lot. He lived a very quiet life and I know he enjoyed coming down to our house to watch the TV at the weekends. I also tell my grandchildren this in London that my uncle had no electricity in his house and they can't believe it, but there were a few people like this who had just a gas mantle in the soo side, not many, but a few, and this is what makes us realise how lucky we are today with all we have.

By this time as I say I'm over nine years old and I'm going back over the toon to Lewis's in Argyle St but it's not for queueing up the back stairs to see Santa in his grotto, no, it's to buy an airfix model of aeroplane's which came in a box and you had to assemble them yourself and stick all the parts together with the wee tube of glue that came with your airfix box. My pal, Dennis Smith and I were into this big time. He had assembled quite a few of these aeroplanes in his house and this is what got me interested. I remember one Saturday morning walking over with him to Lewis's building on Argyle St but because we were on our own the door attendant wouldn't let us in to the store (he must have thought we were going inside to shoplift from the toy department). We explained we had money and wanted to buy an airfix model but to no avail, so not to be deterred we walked round to one of the other doors and waited till the door attendant went inside and as fast as a greyhound we were in the building and made our way up to the toy department. We each bought an airfix model and left Lewis's as pleased as punch with ourselves.

On thinking back I suppose the door attendants were only doing their job, as shoplifting was quite common back then, and not only in Lewis's but the other big stores all over the toon.

In this year of 1957 I was becoming aware of events not only happening around me in the soo side but also worldwide events and a thing called a Sputnik. The sputnik was a spaceship and they had dogs or monkeys in them and I wondered to myself maybe one day they will land on Mars. I remember going to the Ritz Picture House and seeing a film called "Invaders from Mars" and in my youthfulness, I wanted to find out was there any life on that planet as some of the space comics I had bought from "Dirty Maggies shop" on Rutherglen Rd had shown alien life in them. As I was getting older I was getting more knowledgeable or 'nosey' as they say.

I meant to say that round the corner from Moffat St where my pal Dennis Smith lived, there was a shop in Ballater St called the "Shan" or "Shanny" as it was nicknamed. This shop was owned by the Co-op and its claim to fame was it sold broken biscuits, buns, cakes and bread that was a day old, so you could buy them much cheaper and there was always a queue outside of the "Shan." I was sent there a few times to buy some of those items as our mothers were always on the lookout for a bargain, and for sixpence in the old money you could get quite a lot to feed you and the family. More or less over the road you had the massive and beautiful United Co-operative Building Society building (UCBS), which had 24 ovens in it making bread, biscuits and cakes and employed thousands of workers, mainly from the soo side. There were people always working night shift and there always seemed to be many vans parked outside to take all the newly made bread etc to Co-op shops all over Glasgow.

Of course if you followed Ballater St and crossed over the Kings Bridge it took you to where the football pitches were situated at Glasgow Green and who of us can ever forget "The Shows" that came there every year. I think, if I remember correctly, the Shows arrived two weeks before the Glasgow Fair Fortnight and stayed until two weeks after it. How I remember walking over there and looking at the dive bombers, wurlitzers and the big wheel etc and the motor bikes going around and around so fast and it seemed all the girls were screaming with excitement and the pop songs of the day being belting out from all the stalls. There was really such a buzz in the air and even if you had no money to spend it was just magic looking at all the stalls and machines.

Most weans were taken there with their parents and would get a toffee apple or stick of candy floss bought for them, while lots of mothers and grannies would sit down for a game of "housey housey" (bingo) or be a devil and go into "Madame Za Za's" to get their fortune told for a shilling or two. I used to stand with my wee Granny Hendry and her favourite stall was where you rolled an old penny from a wooden chute and if it landed in any of the square boxes then she would get money back. Standing or passing by the stalls, the owners would always be shouting out "C'mon and try your luck," but the one that made me laugh was the stall that had the coconut shy and people used to throw balls at them to knock the coconut off its perch. In all the years that I went over to the Shows I can honestly say that I never saw anybody dislodge one of those coconuts, I think they must have been glued on (ha ha).

Now sometimes at the Shows you would get a few of the street gangs, the Cumbie, the Derry or Tongs etc but there was never really any fighting, it was just a bit of posing and there were usually a couple of polis walking round anyway. It was such a great time going to the Shows and everybody was usually in a great mood. We could have went two different ways, leaving Fauldhouse St and walking down to Polmadie Rd and crossing over the Kay Bridge (later to become known as the Polmadie Bridge and ran from

Polmadie Road over to the football pitches on Fleshers Haugh) was one way, or the other way was walk along Rutherglen Rd, along Waterside St then cross over the King's Bridge. There was only a few minutes walking time difference. What we tended to do was cross over the Kay Bridge, walk all the way throw the Shows (Twice) and cross over the King's Bridge and back onto Rutherglen Rd and always with a poke of chips to share with plenty of salt and vinegar, oh life couldn't have been better!!!

Back to our house and if I ran up the stairs (plenty of energy to burn being a wean) and got to our door first, then I would shove my hand through the letterbox and pull out our door key which was tied to a piece of string. I think most people in the soo side done this. The only time we took the door key away from that piece of string was when we went away for our Fair Fortnight holiday.

Oh the summer months seemed to last forever and how us weans loved the school summer holidays. We would be out playing from first thing in the morning until last thing at night. 'Kick the can' was a favourite game played in the streets or maybe a game of rounders, but all these games would come to a sudden stop if we heard a bugle being played as it meant the rag man was coming. Everyone of us would be running up the stairs (two at a time!!) and begging our ma's for any old clothes that we could give to the rag man. In exchange for the clothes we would get a balloon or a wee toy, but I'm afraid our balloons never lasted that long before they burst or you took them up to your house to play with later and in the morning when you woke up it was deflated. However, it was just the pure excitement of getting the balloon off of the rag man that made you feel like you had been given a million dollars.

I remember all the lassies in the street playing skipping ropes and then some of their mothers joined in too, and they were good. Of course, they would only have been in their early twenties but to me, Mrs Brown and Mrs Kelly seemed "too old" to be doing this but I remember them all laughing while skipping and this was just one feeling of togetherness that gave us this tremendous community spirit that could be found all over the soo side. Most of the people never had a lot of money and I think that this is what drew us all together. If somebody was sick everyone would rally round and all help as best as they could.

In addition, at this time in Glasgow in the mid 1950's, we had terrible smog attacks. This was caused by all the smoke coming out of all the factory chimneys and all our open coal fires in our tenement dwellings. It was so bad sometimes that you could hardly see in front of your face and the buses could only creep along at a snail's pace. Of course this didn't deter us young budding football players, we still played our football in the streets and kicking the ball even though we could hardly see it, now how's that for dedication? Although the Clean Air Act came into force, and slowly over the years the smog attacks disappeared, I will never forget those "pea souper days." I can still taste it in my mouth when I think back and I'm sure you the reader (of my generation), can too.

Another game we played in the tenements was 'kick door run fast.' We used to have one boy standing on each of the three landings, then when the shout went up "Go," each boy chapped (knocked) on each door of the landing he was on which was usually three, then run like the clappers down the stairs. It was usually the boy from the top landing that got caught by one of the people on the bottom landing, but this was the thrill of it all, and sure it was only a bit of fun, although some of the people could be right moaners lol

I am now nearing ten years old and my pal John Doherty (Doc), who broke his leg in Wee Bonnies playground is going to watch Celtic playing at Parkhead. His widowed mother who came from Donegal would take him with her as they walked over to Glasgow Green, through Bridgeton and all the way up London Rd till they reached Parkhead. I asked Mrs Doherty would she take me along with her and she said only if you mammy says yes. I pleaded with my ma, and as she knew Mrs Doherty was a good kindly woman, she agreed.

So there was me now on a Saturday afternoon going to watch my heroes play at football and I felt over the moon. There was another pal of mine called Billy Graham who lived up John Doherty's close and we bumped into him on the stairs, he was going to watch Rangers play at Ibrox as his da was taking him, so we were all in our element. Later on in life I would meet up with Billy as his parents were also moved out to the South Nitshill housing scheme that we moved to.

It's funny you know, but all of us boys who supported different teams all played football together, and where I lived, as I said before, was the 'Steamie' and at the back of the Steamie was a piece of vacant ground or as we called it "the spare grun" and it was here we held our football matches. There could have ended up fifteen aside sometimes as it seems every boy in the soo side was football mad, it was a couple of jumpers for the goalposts and then everybody went at it hammers and tongs, with a lot of hard tackles going in. No prisoners were taken when we held our football matches, and sometimes there was the odd punch up. I know as I tackled one boy one day he punched me, and I, in turn, punched him back, then the two of us were rolling around on the spare grun, but the football match never stopped. Anyway we got up and got stuck back into the match again and the next day we were pals again which is the way it should be, but I think if there had been a referee at our matches he would have ran out of red cards!!

Oh the Steamie had a wall in Wolseley St and it actually backed on to the furnace inside, we all called it the "hoat wa'." It was here especially on the cold winter nights that us boys and girls would stand with our hands behind our backs warming them against the "hoat wa'" while discussing school, football and pop stars etc. Someone would sing a pop song of the day and all of us would join in. There were a few boys and girls who were aged about fourteen or fifteen and they were having a smoke. In those days it wasn't illegal to sell cigarettes to young people and you could go into a shop and ask for a "single" fag, which was usually a Woodbine and if my memory serves me correctly, you bought the single fag and you were always given a match with it and this cost an old penny.

Back in those days there weren't all the health warnings that we have today, If you smoked a cigarette then you were regarded to be "grown up" and not only just the boys, but the lassies too. Woodbine cigarettes seemed to be a big favourite back in those days and then a "tipped cigarette" came on the scene called Kensitas and inside every packet were "coupons" and after you had saved up so many hundreds of these coupons, you could be entitled to a gift from their Kensitas magazine.

Opposite the "hoat wa'" stood a large storeroom for Fullerton and Sons. It was where they stored lots of ironmongery and general wares for houses. My ma used to go there twice a week and keep the place tidy and neat. The Fullertons themselves live in the Muirend area of Glasgow which was classed as a posh area, and my ma also went there every Monday and Friday to clean Mr and Mrs Fullerton's private house. I remember going there once to that house with my ma and couldn't believe they had a big garden in front of their house, two cars, and chandeliers in their living room but most of all soft tissue paper on a toilet roll for their bathroom. Talk about being posh? I remember them as being very nice people and not stand offish. Soft toilet paper, I couldn't believe it, as all we had was the Daily Record or Evening Times cut up into squares for our stairhead lavvy.

Back then in the streets of the soo side you rarely ever saw a car. You may have saw the odd works van but most people never had cars although, that would change from the early to mid sixties, so weans were more or less safe to play in the streets without the fear of being knocked down. There was one guy who used to have a pony and trap and he would have about eight or ten kids sitting in the back of the trap as he drove down Alice St, which had Big Bonnies and Wee Bonnies schools either side of it and for the pricely sum of one old penny, he would drive you up and down the street with all of us weans loving it. I mean we usually walked up or down there all the time, still it was a wee bit of excitement for us, even though it cost our ma's a penny!!

I remember on a Saturday going to Paddy's Market as I have said before, but on a Sunday my pals and me would sometimes take a walk to the "Barras" just past Paddy's market and along the Gallowgate. Well this too was a magic place to go, and even before you got to the Barras, you had different people lining the road selling you, or trying to sell you, their wares. There was this strong armed man who used to put a sack over his head and then get his assistant to chain and padlock him up. His assistant would be saying "The world record stands at so many minutes to get off all these padlocks and chains," then all of a sudden somebody shouted "Look oot the polis is coming" and the strong armed man was free in seconds, running away from the polis. A pure character, but quite strong and I saw him tearing up a phone directory book. Then there was the Indian Oil Snake Man, trying to sell you bottles of his wonder potion or this big African man selling horse racing tips. This all added to the buzz of going over to the Barras on a Sunday afternoon.

Then you had the Barras itself and so jam packed you could hardly move. There were all the patter merchants selling you all kinds of wares like China tea sets, canteens of cutlery sets, rolls of lino, rugs, carpets and everything else you can think of. In fact, people came from all over, not only Glasgow but further afield and even hired buses to take them there. Then who can ever forget the wee monkeys? You paid a shilling or two and you got your photo taken with them, oh the Barras was some place to go.

I suppose us living in the soo side were lucky as we didn't have that far to travel over to the toon. It was only a short walk over from the Suspension Bridge (South Portland St), Victoria bridge, Albert Bridge or St Andrews (Spenny Bridge) and back in those days it seemed we walked everywhere, and yes, it did keep us fit. I remember when going over to the toon with my ma there was always a man sitting down on the pavement just at the Trongate and he would be drawing pictures with chalk and ma would always give him a penny or two while saying to me, "You never know what has happened to that person." My ma was always kind that way, not like today, when I go back to Glasgow on my yearly holiday I see young teenagers sitting with paper cups in their hands begging and they seem to be everywhere.

It was always nice to go over the toon but it was so nice to get back to your tenement house, especially in the winter time and you had the coal fire blazing and sitting down to your dinner. I know in a hundred years time from now that people will still be looking back at the era of the tenements that my generation grew up in. These will be the photos and stories they will be looking at, and maybe people like myself (and many others), who have put our lives and times down in books to explain what it was like, will help them to understand what it was like in our era.

Opposite my house you had Big Bonnies playground and also the Janitors house. Now the Janny of Big Bonnies had a son called Jim Gibb and we got very friendly. The good thing with being the Janny's son was we could play football all night long in the playground with nobody to annoy us. We usually had a two aside headers game with my other pals John Doherty and maybe Brian Donnelly or Mitchell Crombie.

Well Jim was a nice lad as I said, but we were caught by his mother as we had a cigarette in theboiler room one time and I suppose it was a shock for her that two nine year old boys were smoking, although we never really were smokers, we just wanted to try it out and see what it was like. In fact it made me dizzy, but I didn't want to be called 'chicken' but Mrs Gibb said "I'm telling your mother unless you say you won't smoke again!" Well that was it, no more smoking for me, I didn't have to be told twice (ha ha) and what a relief.

I remember as I'm sure lots of you do, our first "mobile phone" in the soo side. It was two empty cans with a hole in the bottom of them that you connected a piece of string, then standing about ten feet apart you shouted into your can to your mate "Can you hear me.?" Well I'm sure the whole bloomin' street could hear us. If we got fed up playing with the "mobile phone" then we would stand on top of the same two cans with string once again attached to them, and as we held the string in our hands we had a pair of stilts!! Oh we were very inventive weans.

I was still being an adventurer and going midgie raking all over the soo side. If it wasn't in the back courts of the Gorbals then I would be midgie raking down through Oatlands and some days you were lucky, other days you weren't, but that was all the excitement of it all. I remember my ma buying me a comic every day, the Dandy, Beano, Topper or whatever, and it was great reading them and swapping them with your pals but I was nearing my tenth birthday and the comics were being overtaken by my love of books. So it was off to McNeil St library for me. I can remember the library ticket I had was about one inch by two inches and had a wee pouch at the bottom where you placed the ticket telling you what book you had borrowed, whereas nowadays it's all electronic stuff.

I would leave McNeil St library and usually took a walk up Snowden St where ma and da had lived when they first got married and thought if they had stayed there and I was born then it would have been right on the doorstep of the library, but such is life and I was just as happy being brought up in Fauldhouse St.

Jokes

This Glasgow man is lying on his deathbed with his wife Mary sitting beside him, he is semi delirious and she is mopping his brow. He comes round and says "Mary hen, I have something to tell you before I pass away." She says "Hush now." He drifts back into slumber but ten minutes later he wakes again and says "Mary hen, I have something to tell you before I die" and Mary says "Hush now , hush now," but Shuggie says "No, I must tell you that I was unfaithful to you three times." Mary says "Hush now, I know." Shuggie says "You know? When did you find out?" and Mary says "Last week, that's why I poisoned ye!"

A wee guy walks into a gentleman's outfitters in Argyle St and the assistant comes over to him and asks if she can help him, the man says "I would like a pair of fur gloves." The assistant say "What fur?" and the guy says "Tae keep mah bloomin hauns warm."

Two pals having a drink in the pub and one says to the other, "So you took sky diving lessons? Did you have any problems?" His pal says "Aye, trying tae keep mah fag lit."

A young lad takes his girlfriend home for the first time and he says to his father, "This is Amanda." His da says "Looks like a lassie tae me son."

What do you call a man who takes a small size in a shoe?
Wee Shoey.

What did Dracula get when he came to Glasgow?
A bat in the mouth.

There was three coos in a field, which wan was on its holidays?
The wan wae the wee calf.

A man walks into a clothes shop and asks the assistant for a maroon jacket. The assistant says "A maroon jacket sir? He says "Aye, to fit maroon shooders."

What do you call a Glasgow Sikh who enjoys Karaoke?
Gupty Singh.

A guy getting ready to go out to the pub says to his wife Ella "Put your hat and coat on." She replies "Aw Tommy, that's nice you're taking me to the pub with you." Tommy says "Naw, I'm switching aff the central heating while I'm oot."

At an art exhibition in Glasgow this wealthy American tourist loses his wallet containing £1,000. He announces to the people gathered there that he would offer £20 to the person who finds it. From the back of the hall comes a voice "I'll give £50."

A wee Glasgow man walks into a greengrocers shop and asks the assistant for a tin of pigeons. The assistant says "Sorry Sir, no can doo."

Wee Tam is in a terrible state and goes to see a private therapist, too terrified to go to see his doctor in case he's declared mad.

"So how can I help says the therapist?"

"It's like this" says wee Tam, "Ah've started getting these fears at night time and they're getting worse. I keep thinking that somebody is under the bed, so in the middle of the night, on the hour, every hour, I get out and look under the bed but there's no one there. Then I go back to bed, but can't get to sleep and keep getting up all night long to see if there's anybody under the bed. I feel as if I'm going mental."

The therapist thinks for a bit and says "I am positive that I can cure you of this. Now I want you to come and see me twice a week for the next six months for a two hour session each time." "How much will that cost me?" asks wee Tam. The therapist says "£60 per session." Wee Tam leaves troubled at all that amount of money he will have to pay and goes to his local pub for a drink.

The therapist never sees Tam again until months later he bumps into him in the street and the therapist is surprised to see Tam looking so well and cheerful, not the sleep deprived maniac that he'd seen before.

"Why did you never come back to see me?" he asks wee Tam.

"Well at £60 a pop, twice a week for six months you must be kidding. The barman at my local pub cured me for £10."

"How on Earth did he do that?" asked the therapist. Tam said "He told me to buy a saw and cut the legs aff the bed!!"

**Glasgow Court Story - This is apparently a true story.
The scene is a Glasgow court and a witness (a ned) is being questioned by a rather plummy mouthed Solicitor!
Solicitor: "You say you went up to your friends house that night. Why did you go there?"
Accused: "Tae get a tap."
Solicitor: "Is your friend a plumber?"
Accused: "Naw."
Solicitor: "Are you a plumber?"
Accused: "Naw"
The accused is a bit bewildered by this line of questioning and the Solicitor realises it, but notices that the court police officer is rubbing the fingers of one hand together in the universal gesture of money. Daylight apparently dawns on the Solicitor and he changes his line of questioning accordingly.
Solicitor: "So you went to the house to borrow money?"
Accused: "Naw."
Solicitor: "Ah. You went to the house to lend money?"
Acused: "Naw."
In exasperation the Solicitor says, "You told the court you went to your friend's house for a tap. What kind of tap was it?"
Accused: "A Celtic tap."**

River Clyde and Rutherglen Road - early 1960's

Gorbals - early 1960's

Oatlands- early 1960's

Lewis's Argyle Street - 1950's

Lawmoor Street - October 1962

Adelphi Terrace Secondary - February 1960

Chapter 5

The year is now 1958 and I'm ten years old and I know that I'm growing up because it used to be on a Friday night (or the weekend) that my ma used to get the old tin bath in from the hall lobby, fill it with boiling water from the kettle and give my sister and me a bath in front of the coal fire. My sister went in first then came out and then it was my turn and the water was never that hot, while your ma washed your back with that bloomin' hard scrubbing brush. This was a ritual that happened all over the soo side and I'm sure that you, the reader, if you're of my generation will remember it well. Nobody can say they have ever lived if they never stood in front of the coal fire drying yourself after coming out of the old tin bath. As I say, I knew I was getting older because this weekly ritual stopped and my ma gave me money to go over to the steamie and have a hot bath on a Friday after I had finished school.

I would cross over our street and pay my money for the hot bath at the cashier's window, getting my ticket and a flimsy towel with a cake of carbolic soap and walk upstairs and sit down on a bench, and wait my turn till one of the baths was ready. I always remember it was pretty packed with people waiting to get a bath on a Friday evening. I was usually the only boy there and the rest were men who were probably getting all cleaned and ready for going out later that night for a drink and maybe a visit to the dance hall as it was a Friday and they had been paid.

The bath attendant would clean out the bath from its previous occupant and then shout out "Right who's next?" When it was my turn then off I'd go and enter my cubicle, undress and go into my bath. The attendant filled your bath up from outside your cubicle with a turnkey and once you were in the bath he would knock your door and ask you if you wanted more hot water or cold. He only ever asked you the once and that was it, oh it was great, just laying there, there were glass panels in the roof so you had plenty of light. One memory of mine sticks out more than others and that was the attendant had a radio always turned on and this day Buddy Holly was singing "That'll be the day" and as I was washing myself with the bar of carbolic soap I thought "This is pure magic," although that smell of carbolic has never left me, even to this day I can still smell it.

Then a knock on the door meant your allocated time was up, so you stood up on a wooden duck board and dried yourself with the flimsy towel you had been given, but boy oh boy did you feel good. The attendant emptied your dirty water, cleaned the bath and started filling it for the next customer. I remember on the wall on the way out there was a Brylcream machine and for two penny's old money you got a dollop of it from a nozzle. I watched a few men doing this, and there was a mirror on the wall so the men could comb their Brylcreamed hair into place, I wasn't in to that (yet). Oh how great the feeling was when you walked out into the street after your hot bath, but as I say the smell of that bloomin' carbolic soap was the only let down.

My parents had allowed me to go with Mrs Doherty and her son John (Doc) to go and see Celtic play but some Saturdays when it was a home game she didn't go, which meant in turn I couldn't go either. What I did do though was tell my ma I was off to see Clyde Football Club play their home match at Shawfield Park, but what I did was walk myself up to Parkhead, get a lift over to see my team play but fifteen minutes before the match ended the gates opened and I ran like the clappers all the way back to Shawfield Park and caught up with the people coming out of it and asked them the final score so I could tell my ma when I got home. I know it was naughty of me but that's the way it happened.

Another of the things that stays in my memory was Dixon's Blazes Ironworks. The whole sky in the soo side was lit up at night time with all the sparks and flashes of molten iron being poured into casts. It was like the Northern Lights (auroras boreales) and you could watch it for ages. Sadly in this year, 1958, Dixon's blazes closed down due to a recession and the foundry was being dismantled. The news spread around that the great big brick chimney was going to be blown up with a dynamite charge. So as a ten year old boy I stood with loads of neighbours at the top of Alice

St, with Big Bonnies one side of the street and Wee Bonnies the other side. Then there was the explosion and down the chimney came to a great big cheer, but it was sad really when I think back because this was part of the south side's history being taken away, just the same way that in years to come that the multi storie buildings in the Gorbals would be taken down, sad, but never the less part of our history.

Earlier that year I was in my house when a knock went at the door and my ma went to answer it and it was two lassies, Connie Beattie and her pal Elizabeth, who actually lived in the same close as my Granny Hendry. Now they handed my ma an envelope and ran down our stairs laughing. I wondered what it was that my ma was handing me and when I opened it up it was a handmade Valentine's Day card from Connie. I didn't know what to say. It had a few words written on it which I forget now but there were plenty of kisses on it. I was only ten years old so I wasn't in to any of that thing, of course as the years changed and I grew older then I did. That was the only Valentine's Day card that I have ever received in my life so I will never forget it, although I sent a few of my own in years to come to some lassies that I fancied.

This was the year that Elvis Presley joined the US army and of all the singers on the pop scene and there were quite a few that I liked, I have to say that Elvis was my favourite and I loved to hear him belt out all the rock n roll songs and if you went into one of the many cafes/ice-cream parlours that covered the whole of the soo side, then you were sure to hear an Elvis song being played. In Glasgow at that time you had the "Teddy Boys" who wore those lovely drape jackets and crepe sole shoes. There were a few fights that I remember involving the Teddy Boys or "Teds" as they were sometimes called, although I must say I think they always looked smart wearing all their clothes and "DA" combed hair, some people said they were a symptom of the rock n roll era. The "DA" was reported to come from America and stand for "District Attorney," although we sometimes called it the "Duck's arse!"

As I said, I'm ten years old and in my last class before the dreaded eleven plus exam which would determine whether we went to a Junior Secondary or a Senior Secondary School. Our class teacher Mr Jimmy D'Arcy had told us that he too was leaving Wee Bonnies School to go teach in another part of Glasgow and us his pupils were all sorry to be seeing him go, even though we wouldn't be in Wee Bonnies either after the eleven plus exam. Miss Martin one of our other teachers and a nice lady asked us would we like to all chip in some money to buy Mr D'Arcy a farewell present (well the money would come from our parents).

Over the course of many months we had given a fair amount of money for Mr D'Arcy's farewell present and now Miss Martin said "Right, I will take two pupils with me over to the town and we'll choose a nice going away present for Mr D'Arcy and the person who has donated the most money will come with me." This happened to be my pal, Dennis Smith and he was given the task to put his hand in a bucket that had everybody's name in it and pull out the name of the person who would join him. He put his hand in the bucket and pulled out my name, but a few of the other pupils said it wasn't fair as me and him were best pals. Miss Martin said "Right then Dennis, I will put Daniel's name back into the bucket, give it a good shake and you can pick once again" and this seemed to placate the others who were complaining. Well would you believe it? Dennis only went and pulled my name out again!! Miss Martin said "That's fair enough," although I could hear a few murmurs, so I said I wouldn't go and let Dennis pick again but this time she was quite adamant, my name had been drawn and that was the end of the matter.

I always remember that Miss Martin took Dennis and me over to the Argyle Arcade and we chose a pipe for Mr D'Arcy's going away present and we presented it to him just before he left St Bonaventure's school and he thanked all of our class as one for giving him such a nice present. Later on in life when I became a bricklayer I was on a building site in the Thornliebank area of Glasgow when I was working alongside a bricklayer called John D'Arcy and lo and behold he was only the brother of my old teacher

Mr Jimmy D'Arcy, now how's that for a coincidence? Anyway, that following Saturday (we worked till twelve noon) John said he was meeting up with his brother Jimmy in one of the bars in the Toon before they went to the football and would I like to come along. I surely did and although this was nine years later since I had last saw him, I knew him straight away and I was still calling him Mr D'Arcy. He said "Please call me Jimmy," and I did, but it didn't feel right somehow. We had a great old talk about Wee Bonnies and this all came about because I happened to be working alongside his brother John, what a great day that was.

I was still going to the Gorbals swimming baths. Sometimes I would go with some of my pals or sometimes I would go on my own and having learnt to swim by now I didn't have any fear of being pushed in again. My ma had bought me a swimming mask with a snorkel attached to it and I would be swimming full lengths of the baths but the other boys didn't half take the mickey out of me wearing a snorkel mask that I never took it again. I clearly remember one day coming out of the swimming baths and walking into Bedford Lane (at the side of the baths) where Lipton's Memorial Sculptures had a little yard displaying graveside headstones with wording and dates on them. I stood there looking at them, and as I did I thought to myself "What will it be like when it's the year is 2000, Jeezo, I'll be fifty two years old" but that was so far in the future for a young boy to try and imagine and I also thought that I'd be ancient by that time (ha ha). Well now as I write my story today the year is 2016 and I'm sixty eight years old, but I certainly don't feel ancient. I've just been round the block a few times!!

I always remember that Gorbals Cross was a busy intersection and loads of people going for their messages. It had so many shops and cafes and anytime if I needed the toilet then there was one just at the Cross. You went downstairs to this and I clearly remember that wee brass box on the toilet door where you inserted a penny to use the cubicle, there was a man who actually looked after the toilet there and kept the place spotless and there were those glass blocks on the pavement above to give a bit of daylight, although the glass blocks were that thick no one could ever see through them. In fact there were quite a few of these toilets spread all over Glasgow at that time, but with the Gorbals clearance they disappeared.

I could never get over the amount of pubs that there were in the greater Gorbals area, it seemed they were everywhere you looked. I always wished that I was grown up and working and going in for a pint of beer after I'd finished work on a Friday night. Oh yes, I remember passing the pubs doors on a Friday night and if the door was open you could see the place was packed. Unfortunately thought, I also saw some women standing outside the pubs doors in the hope that their husband would come out soon and come home before squandering their hard earned wages. That was one thing about my own da, every Friday he came straight home with his wage packet unopened. When I grew up myself, I would like a drink and I suppose it was/is a weakness of mine although I could handle it as opposed to some poor souls who let it get a grip of them.

Friday nights was a great night for the fish and chip shops as I'm sure you, the reader, will agree with, and there were so many of them. We all had our favourite one whatever part of the soo side we lived and the thing was, back in those days, as I've said before, they were all wrapped up in newspaper and I don't know why, but they seemed to taste better. A special fish supper and maybe a picked onion, oh man, you just couldn't beat it. Of course this was the night us weans got our pocket money. Your da gave your ma his wages and your ma in turn gave you your pocket money and you just couldn't wait to go and see the Saturday matinee pictures and have a few sweeties while watching the films.

Of course, as I was getting older the Saturday morning pictures didn't hold the same draw for me, I still liked going to the pictures but I was now playing for my school football team, Wee Bonnies, and every Saturday morning we played other teams in our league over on Glasgow Green. I think the area where the football was played was called Fleshers Haugh, the word fleshers was an old word for butchers and haugh is a low lying piece of ground near a river.

All the football pitches (actually just ash and no grass at all) were fully booked up with all the school football teams playing there. If you were unlucky enough to have came off second best in a tackle and cut your leg the ash would go into it and it could be very sore. There was a pavilion where you could have a shower after your match, but they were always packed, so you had to go home and try and wash your cut leg or arm clean. I played in the right full back position but have to be honest and say I was only a fair player, none of the big Glasgow football clubs came to sign me (ahhhh).

I do remember a match we played one Saturday morning and the opposing team were awarded a penalty against us as I had fouled one of the opposing team players in our penalty area. Our goalkeeper, Mitchell Crombie, stood there in goal and I was praying into myself "Come on Mitchell, please save it, please save it" as I would get the blame for costing us a goal. Anyway Mitchell did save it, but as he dived to stop the ball it hit him on the side of his head. As a result of this, Mitchell was knocked out as the player who took the kick hit it so hard and the ball went at a tremendous pace all the way down the grass bank and into the River Clyde. The game had to be abandoned as we had no replacement ball, ah well at least we never lost.

So the Glasgow Green had quite a few things going on for it over the years. The shows as I mentioned before, the football pitches and just over the other side of the King's Bridge you had the open gymnasium. The gymnasium held all sorts like the parallel bars, the hand rests on chains where you could pull yourself up and other exercising apparatus, only I'm not sure if they're there anymore. Then we had the People's Palace and the Winter Gardens where so many of us soo siders could take a walk and spend a very interesting and informative day. As I said earlier, us soo side people were lucky really being so close to Glasgow Green and the toon and not forgetting the River Clyde with the rowing boats. On the point of the River Clyde, I always remember walking over to or past the King's Bridge and the smell coming from the whiskey bonded warehouse on Ballater St, oh what an aroma. Then there was that row of single storey houses all along Waterside St just on the banks of the Clyde. I actually think these houses were built in between the wars as the majority of the three storied tenements were built in the mid - late nineteenth century and further back to Snowden St you also had these one story high houses where my ma and da first lived when they married.

Now the time is drawing near for the dreaded eleven plus school exams which would take us to either a Junior or Senior Secondary School but before we had that we had our last Christmas school party with crisps, buns and ginger all supplied and every one of us weans enjoying ourselves. Once again our star singer was the terrific Geana Sweeney (McPike) who belted out a few Elvis Presley songs. No one realises how happy your school days were unfortunately, until you yourself look back, on them although at the time you don't see it that way.

Now I am eleven years old and have sat the eleven plus exam and I failed it, which means that I will now be going to St Bonaventure's Junior Secondary School and not Holyrood Senior Secondary School where my pals Dennis Smith and Brian Donnelly are going after gaining top marks.

My ma had always wanted me to go to Holyrood School as like all mothers she wanted the best for her wean but in my case it wasn't to be, so off to Big Bonnies I went. It was a school of hard knocks and it toughened you up with most of the teachers there being "belt" or "strap" mad." The majority of the boys there came from the Gorbals, only a short distance away, and quite a few of the older ones were members of the "Cumbie" street gang with most coming from Cumberland St area or surrounding streets and were nobody's fool to say the least.

In fact with me being a pal of Jim Gibb (whose da was the janny of Big Bonnies School) well one Saturday he took us into the schoolmaster Mr Berry's room and opened up a cupboard that was full of knives, knuckle dusters and studded belts that had been confiscated off of members of the Cumbie and the amount was massive. No wonder they were one of the most feared street fighting gangs, not only in the soo side but in Glasgow itself. One of the Cumbie members was called Jimmy Boyle who went onto become a gangster and was tried on murder charges a few times before he was put away in jail for many years. He was absolutely ruthless and knew no fear. I'm glad to say that when in prison and after settling down after being involved in riots he turned over a new leaf. He married and now leads a peaceful life doing sculpturing works, he wrote a book called " A Sense of Freedom " which was made into a film shown on TV.

There was one teacher called Mr Lee or "Scud Lee" as we called him he would carry his strap over his shoulder ready to give the strap to any boy who he thought had misbehaved. Cowboys in the western films carried their guns at their side ready for action but this Scud Lee carried his strap on his shoulder ready for action. The reason he was called Scud Lee was a lot of times instead of giving you the strap he would wrap his knuckles over your forehead or scud (with his hand) the back of your head and it was bloomin' sore, I can personally vouch for that.

Of course there were other teachers who weren't as vicious as Scud Lee and one in particular that I recall was a Mr Vaughan who we nicknamed "Frankie" after Frankie Vaughan the singer and stage performer who was all the rage in the late 1950's and all through the 60's. He was our English teacher and in our free periods in class he would read us Treasure Island straight from the book and he would put a different accent on for each character that he was imitating and it had us boys all enthralled.

There were other teachers in Big Bonnies and one called Mr Morgan was a dead ringer for the Celtic Football Club's centre forward called Steve Chalmers, so we all nicknamed him "Stevie" but he was another teacher who was too fond of giving you the strap. Mr McLaughlin was our geography teacher and a nice man who didn't give you the belt at all, he had a way with words that made you behave in the classroom, in fact he used to put on a racing bet with my uncle, Wullie Glasgow at dinner time.

Big Bonnies was, as I say, not a school for the faint hearted, in fact like a lot of schools they had boys going round in wee gangs trying to bully you and if they spotted a "new" boy who had just joined the school, then they would give him the initiation welcome, which was for them to grab you bodily by the arms and legs and swing you up and over a six feet high wall that had an open space of ground that actually abutted on to the gable end of my tenement. When this happened to me I landed on a few broken bricks and was lucky not to have broken any bones but at least I had been "initiated" and wouldn't be thrown over the wall again!!

In the boys toilet here in Big Bonnies it was like entering a smoke screen as it seems everyone was smoking a cigarette or sharing one. As I said, at that time in the late 1950's you could walk into any newsagents and buy a "single" which was a loose cigarette and a match to light it. The newsagents shops all around Bonnies must have made a fortune selling all these "single fags." Of course every now and then the teachers would have a purge and rush into the boys toilets and capture the ones who were smoking or who weren't fast enough to throw their cigarette away, they would be marched off to the headmaster Mr Berry's office, given a telling off and also six of the best from the teacher's belt but that didn't deter the smokers, in fact it kind of gave them "street cred."

One claim to fame I have of attending Big Bonnies is my ma's kitchen/living room window overlooked its playground and at playtime if ma wasn't working then I would shout up to her window for a jeely piece (if I was still hungry after eating the one she had wrapped up for me before I went to school that day). My ma would dutifully do this and throw it down into the playground where I would quickly eat it. Our tenement window and my uncle Wullie Glasgow's windows were the only two windows that looked down in to Big Bonnies playground, so I had to be the only boy that ever had a jeely piece thrown down to him in the lifetime of Big Bonnies school.

There were a few fights in the playground and I'm talking about no holds barred punching and kicking and using a metal studded belt while everyone seemed to form a ring round the two fighters. The shout went up "fight" "fight" then the teacher who was supervising the playtime break would come rushing in and try and break it up, although sometimes the fighters would turn on him until other teachers came to break it all up, this meant another trip to the headmaster's office and on some occasions the fighters were expelled from the school which in their eyes saw their "street cred" soar!!

Now with the year being 1959, I noticed my ma changing from being the happy person she always was into a person who started swearing sometimes (I had never heard my ma swear before) and would stay in bed some days. I couldn't make it out. My da pulled me aside and said "I'll tell you when you're older son it's called woman's trouble." My da never did tell me what it was, it was the same as he said he would tell me about the facts of life but he never did, I think he was more embarrassed than me. It was the "change of life " that my ma was going through that I later found out and in those far off days there was no HRT so women like my ma went through this without any real help. In fact it took the best part of fifteen years for my ma to get back to the way she used to always be and it left me as an eleven year old boy confused as some days my ma would be fine other days she would be shouting at me and my sister.

I remember a great cowboy programme being on the television at the time it was called 'Bonanza' about Ben Cartwright and his three sons, Adam, Hoss and little Joe and all the different adventures they would get up to. Everybody in the soo side was talking about it and it had a fabulous instrumental tune that would have you "playing it with your hands on an imaginary guitar" and we all discussed it at school or when outside. Now fifty seven years later as I write my book, I have the pleasure on a Saturday night to watch re-runs of the show on Freeview TV and yes, I sit there pretending to play my guitar.

Also at this time we had a craze all over Glasgow and it was called a "hula hoop," a piece of plastic tubing shaped as a ring and the idea/craze was to gyrate your body side to side and try and keep the hula hoop moving in a fast spin. Everybody was playing it in the streets and houses of the soo side and we even held competitions in the back courts to see who could keep the hula hoop going for the longest. We also had the yo-yo craze and you had some weans who were brilliant at "walking the dog" or "going around the world." I was never any good at it but some other weans as I say were brilliant.

On the pop music scene at the time we had a young Cliff Richard singing Living Doll, Bobby Darin, Connie Francis and a rake of other singers and I always thought that the music from say 1954 up to 1960 was the best music ever. I know that the 60's would have the Beatles and all the other groups which would be fantastic but I loved the 50's music and would love to hear all the lassies singing them as they held their back court concerts. Some of those lassies were really good to listen to, of course Elvis was still in the army but he would come out as good as ever.

Now as I say I'm eleven years old and because I have started secondary school I am now allowed to go to Parkhead on my own and watch Celtic play while a few of my pals who were Rangers supporters and had also started their secondary school were allowed to go to Ibrox to watch their team play. Between going for a hot bath in the steamie on a Friday night and being allowed to go and watch my team play at Parkhead I feel I am getting older and liking it I must say.

Now a strange thing happens to me at Big Bonnies, when the exam time comes along after the first six months I am top of the class, so I am moved up to a higher class and lo and behold six months later when the next exam time comes around I am top of the class again. My ma is over the moon and goes to see the headmaster Mr Berry at Bonnies. He says this has never happened before and he says because of being top of the class twice he would like me to go and spend my last three years at Holyrood, the Senior Secondary School. When the school prizes were being given out I was given the book 'Moby Dick' by Herman Melville and a few words written by the headmaster on the inside leaf.

Another strange quirk of fate is that the boy who came second in the exam was a pal of mine from Wee Bonnies called Peter Donachy who came from Rosyth St, at the very far end of Oatlands (close to Shawfield stadium). He had actually got top marks in the eleven plus exam and was entitled to go to Holyrood Senior Secondary but because his older brother or his cousin was attending Big Bonnies he refused to go to Holyrood, and here is me that wanted to go to Holyrood after the eleven plus exam but couldn't because of low marks, now finding myself in this position. Strange but true, but things like this would happen to most of us as we made our way through our adult lives to come whether we stayed living in the soo side or ventured farther afield.

Just before we had the second exam test in Big Bonnies, one of the teachers came over to me and asked me would I like to go to France the following summer in a school exchange holiday. I went home and told my ma and she said "Yes." There was about nine months to go before we went to give our parents time to pay money every week for the holiday. However, my ma paid the total money straight away and it was because ma had paid the money in full that it was decided that although I would be a pupil in Holyrood, I would still be allowed to go on the trip to France and I was very grateful for this. Just imagine, me a wean from the soo side was going over to France, oh it was so exciting.

So just after the new year of 1960 I would make my daily trip up to Holyrood School. I was put in a 'prep' class for the first six months before I could go into one of the year classes. It was great to meet up with my old pal Dennis Smith again and yes, once again, I was playing football with him again in the school playground yard.

Chapter 6

Every morning now I pass by my old school, Big Bonnies in Fauldhouse St. I walk up to the top of Fauldhouse St then turn left into Kilbride St and walk along it until I come to Polmadie Rd where I turn right up past the Polmadie engine sheds onto the Malls Mire and into Holyrood Senior Secondary School wearing my school blazer, long trousers and shirt and school tie. I walk this way every morning and also in the afternoon when school is over and on my return journey I stand at the Polmadie railway/road bridge and lean over as the steam engines pass by and catch all the steam in my face, and that smell of the old steam engines has stayed with me all these years. When the steam engine had passed then I would sometimes stand on the bridge and look all over the Oatlands area, as at this point of Polmadie Rd it had a high viewing point. All those lovely red sandstone tenement buildings of Toryglen St, Roseberry St and Dalmeny St etc then Wolseley St in the other direction as Oatlands went onto merge with Gorbals at the near end of Caledonia Rd and I would think to myself how lucky I was to be brought up in this area with all the great people I knew and our fantastic community spirit.

I remember in this year 1960 walking along Rutherglen Rd one Saturday just before coming to the Gorbals Burial Ground or "the Rosie" as we called it and I was looking at the new buildings having their foundations laid. This was to be the Queen Elizabeth Square tower blocks (multi stories) known as Hutchensontown A, B and C designed by Sir Basil Spence. These and other multi story blocks of flats were to replace the old tenements that were being demolished, but as I said before, the idea was new and they were to be the buildings of the future, but sadly, with dampness and structural faults over thirty years later they too were being demolished. Lots of people from the soo side were shipped out to new housing schemes on the outskirts of Glasgow whether it be Toryglen, Castlemilk or Drumchapel etc. Some people didn't want to leave the tenements where they were born and bred while others were looking forward to it. Some others stayed in the Gorbals until the new buildings had been erected and then moved into their new homes with Oatlands Regeneration following suit a few years down the line.

Being twelve years old I was now starting to go to the barbers and noticing all the different hairstyles you could have. It seemed a lot of boys a few years older than me were asking for a "Tony Curtis" or "Perry Como" haircut and that sure beat the "bowl" cut I used to have when I was younger. I remember one night standing up one of the tenement closes with boys and girls a few years older than me, the boys would be combing their "Tony Curtis" hairstyles while some lassies were looking at themselves from a compact mirror and everyone singing the hit song "Tell Laura I Love Her" by Ricky Valance and it was great until one of the neighbours came out and chased us all away (Weren't they young once?) This was a slow ballad song and I don't think we were making too much noise, just as well we weren't singing "My Old Man's a Dustman" by Lonnie Donegan as that would have sounded loud.

I remember I was just starting to take notice of girls although I was very shy. If there was any talk of romance then I would blush if there was any girls about, but I liked listening to all the stories from the older boys and their exploits, probably a load of make believe. However, in my eyes as a twelve year old I wished that I was as old as them and done what they had done. Of course through the years to come I would have a few romantic stories to tell myself but not just yet.

So back at my new school Holyrood and in my prep class, the teachers didn't seem to be so bad or fanatical about giving you the belt as the teachers did in Big Bonnies and that was good, although some of the teachers would give you "lines" if you had been misbehaving. If you were caught talking in class then the teacher would say "Right boy, take two hundred lines 'I must not talk in class when the teacher is talking' and give them to me tomorrow morning." So that night you had to go home and write down "I must not talk in class when the teacher is talking" two hundred times. Sometimes when we had homework classes in the school after ordinary school hours were over, I would write these lines out while pretending to be doing homework and just hope that I wasn't caught, otherwise it would have meant more lines. There was a teacher here in Holyrood whose name was Mr Bob Crampsey and he was a sports commentator on the television show 'Scotsport' and along with the main presenter Arthur Montford, they presented this twice weekly show of all the Scottish sport, but mainly football.

It wasn't uncommon for us boys to whistle the 'Scotsport' TV theme tune if we saw Bob Crampsey in the playground, but he would quickly turn round and give us all lines. I remember I was sitting in his class one day and he gave me three hundred lines for something I had done. Well, this happened on a Friday and every Friday night I would walk to Parkhead to watch the Celtic reserves play underneath the new floodlights that had been installed in the ground, and I kept putting off the lines that I had to hand to Mr Crampsey on Monday morning, well to cut a long story short I never did the lines over the weekend and when I got into school on Monday morning I started writing out the lines, but there was no way I would have them finished when the nine o'clock bell went. So the going rate in Holyrood at that time was you paid a pal a penny to do one hundred lines for you, so I got two of my pals to do one hundred lines each for me which cost me two pennies out of my school dinner money that ma had given me and we just managed to get the lines done in time before the bell rang. I gave Mr Crampsey the three hundred lines all written in different handwriting and he just took them and threw them in the litter bin. What???!!!. Thinking back now to getting lines, I would rather have had the belt as it would have been over in a minute but that's "hard lines" as they say.

Going to Holyrood had an added advantage too because the National Stadium at Hampden Park was only a few minutes' walk away. If there happened to be an International match being played midweek with a three o'clock kick off, then we could go and see the last fifteen minutes being played as the gates always opened at that time to let the crowds get out early if they wanted to, so this is what a lot of us boys from Holyrood done. In addition, just before Hampden Park you had Cathkin Park, which was the home of Third Lanark Football Club or the "Hi Hi" as they were nicknamed, and if they were playing a Scottish cup midweek replay match, we could see the last fifteen minutes there too. Oh yes, this was fantastic for us young lads.

At this time in my life I was still taking walks along Cumberland St because I did love all those shops, although slowly but surely, the tenements were being demolished and it seemed kind of strange as it must have done for other people, that streets you had known all your life were now disappearing. In some places you could actually see into the half demolished tenements and all the different wallpaper in each room that had been put up lovingly over the years, and you would think of all the happy and maybe sad times that ordinary people like me and you had endured, the open coal fires no longer lit and no more smoke coming from the chimneys, it seemed surreal. I had a school pal of mine from Holyrood called James Gilfedder and he came from Norfolk St, just past Gorbals Cross and sometimes I would walk along to his house to play out with him and I always remember his father saying to me he couldn't wait till they knocked down his tenement as they had been earmarked for moving to the new housing scheme at Castlemilk. I wasn't like that at all, as I loved my house in Fauldhouse St.

I must say that I'm happy at my new school and we get taught French too into the bargain. Our French teacher is a Mr McMillan although he has the nickname "Bub," but he is a very nice teacher and full of fun. I remember one day in class he was teaching us a French song "Sur Le Pon Davingon" which translated means "On The Bridge of Avingon." Anyway, we finished singing it and he says "No no, you got to swing it" and he sang it like a rock n roll song. I liked Mr McMillan. Now my prep class is over, we have the exam and I'm sixth from the top of the class and I am put into class 1 Alpha but I don't start there until the summer holidays are over.

Now is the time for adventure and my school holiday excursion over in France but with Big Bonnies, and not Holyrood. My ma buys me my first ever long trouser suit and I feel all grown up and remember the day we left for France was on a Friday and the sun was shining. My da was working on a site for MDW up at Parliamentary

Rd in the toon and ma took me there to show me off to da wearing my first suit. Well da wishes me well and ma takes me back to the Central Station where our train leaves from and I think this is great, me a wee boy from the soo side is going to another country, my stomach was full of butterflies. I had a suitcase with a change of clothes like all the other boys and girls who were going on the journey. My ma and other mothers are there seeing their weans off and we are chaperoned by a few of the school teachers from Big Bonnies. The train went to Dover where we would get the ferry over to France and a connecting train to take us the French school in Versailles, close to Paris.

Off all us boys and girls went, and you can imagine all the chatter. We had all brought a packed lunch made by our mothers as instructed to by the letter our parents had received form Big Bonnies. I fully remember sitting on an aisle seat and sitting opposite me on the other side of the aisle was a girl called Elizabeth and we all started singing the Petula Clark song "Sailor Stop your Roaming." This was number one in the hit parade at the time. Then Elizabeth reached over and held my hand and a feeling I had never experienced before happened, I didn't know what or how to explain this feeling but I sure knew that I liked it and I held hands with Elizabeth for the rest of the journey with the teacher in charge of us looking on, but only smiling.

Then we got on the ferry and connecting train and found ourselves in the school dormitory in Versailles. We were taken into Paris by our teachers who I must say were very good at speaking French and we were taken to the Louvre and saw the portrait of the Mona Lisa, and yes, her eyes did seem like they were following you. Then off up to the Eiffel Tower and right up to the top but it had barbed wire all around it as a lot of people had committed suicide by jumping off of the top. After that we were taken to Notre Dame Cathedral were we attended Mass. We had a great two weeks there and this was the first time I had ever tasted coffee, but more exciting than that was because it was France we could have a glass of wine with our meal. Over twelve and a half years old and I experienced alcohol for the first time. "Viva la France."

Soon our holiday in France was over but what a brilliant two weeks we had. On the way back on the train to Glasgow I was looking for Elizabeth as I had enjoyed holding her hand so much, but to my compete dismay she was sitting holding another boys hand (I think this was a portent of what lay ahead for me later in my love life) (ha ha). I brought back a few wee statues of the Eiffel Tower as presents for my family. My ma was at the Central Station to meet me and asked how I had enjoyed it and I said "Great ma."

When I start back school at Holyrood I'm actually moved to the annexed part of the school on Aikenhead Rd which was much nearer to Hampden Park. There was another boy from Fauldhouse St who went to Holyrood, a James McFadden, and sometimes we would walk up Polmadie Rd together, and to our dislike we used to meet one of our teachers called Mr Keaney, who was eccentric to say the least. He lived somewhere in Bridgeton and if you didn't salute him when you saw him he would give you the belt when you got into school. He was our science teacher but I think he was slightly mad.

So life for me at this time was great, I was three months off of my thirteenth birthday, going to the steamie on a Friday night for a hot bath, waking over to Parkhead to see my team play, playing football in the streets with all my pals and the only drawback was my ma going through this change of life, which as I said I didn't really understand but because I loved my ma I would let it go. My big sister Jeanette had started work in the Twomax Knitwear Factory and in a few months time I would become a teenager so overall life was good.

Then total disaster. I came home from school one day and there were policemen and firemen everywhere. What could have happened? It seemed that the back elevation of our tenement building had collapsed, due to a bit of subsidence in the ground. There were firemen in our back court and they were using massive timbers to shore up that part of our tenement that had collapsed, and to save any more masonry collapsing and in general to prop up the existing walls. We were allowed to stay in our house because it was the other side of the landing that was unsafe, all the neighbours on that side had to go and stay with relatives or friends, as it was too dangerous to live there in case more of the building collapsed. All the emergency services worked into the night trying to shore our tenement up and they had all these great big arc lights switched on all night long.

My family were given two weeks' notice to choose between three housing schemes to move to. My ma and da chose South Nitshill, I had never heard of the place and didn't want to leave the soo side and all my pals and my granny so I said "Can't we stay somewhere else in the soo side?" but with the Gorbals clearance now gathering up speed this didn't seem to be an option. There was a neighbour of ours called Andrew Ewing and he lived in a single end on the landing above us, the ironic thing for him was a month earlier he had won a few hundred pounds on the football pools and he got my uncle Hughie to wallpaper and paint his wee house. When this was all finished he had said knowing my luck the building will now fall down and it did!! Ah poor Mr Ewing.

We were allowed to stay in our house but only for the two weeks, so that Saturday my da had got the keys for this new house of ours and we went to South Nitshill and put newspapers down on the wooden floorboards (this was to be the underlay for our carpet). Our new house was one storey high and had four people in each close. All the three other people came from Govan and they were nice enough, but we never really got to know them that well. My ma was told that we couldn't bring pets with us and that was heart breaking because 'Dandy,' our cat, wasn't allowed to come with us to our new house. I remember walking with my big sister to the Veterinary Surgeon in Gorbals St with Dandy our cat in a basket and she was "put to sleep" and that really upset me. To make matters worse, when we did move to South Nitshill it looked like everyone had brought their pets with them, there were cats and dogs everywhere, poor old Dandy.

On that first Saturday when da and me went to our new house for the first time, we caught a red bus from Clyde St going to a place called Neilston, and it passed through this place called Nitshill. We left the terminus in Clyde St and travelled down Bridge St then Eglinton St up past Queens Park which I had heard of, and a place called Shawlands, which was an upmarket area with nice houses. We then went up through Thornliebank then to this place called Nitshill. When we got off the bus we had a good ten minute walk 'til we came to our new house. This housing scheme was only half built and there was mud everywhere and I just didn't like it, and for the seven years that I stayed there before I started all my travels, I still never took to the place. That's why I was always going back down to visit the soo side.

I remember going back to the soo side and telling all my pals that we had moved to South Nitshill and jokingly said we have two houses, our tenement here and a new house in South Nitshill. My parents were given two weeks free of paying rent in our tenement and the new house but the rent had to be paid starting in two weeks time and onwards, that was no problem as my ma was always a good housekeeper and looked over the family finances splendidly. Then the big day arrived and a furniture van drove into Fauldhouse St and started to take all our furniture downstairs and put it in to the van. All our neighbours were standing there and when all our furniture was in the van all the neighbours waved us off.

What an awful empty feeling there was in my stomach that Saturday. I was the last one out of our house and closed the door behind me. I couldn't believe we were leaving the place that had been my home since I had been brought there as a newly born baby. I also wondered how must have all the other neighbours felt when it was soon their time to move away to go to one of these new housing schemes? My ma, da, sister and me all sat in the back of this furniture van with our belongings and about an hour later we drove up to 39 Willowford Rd, which would be my new home for the next seven years. All our furniture was put in our new home, the furniture removers drove away and we started putting carpets down, curtains up and after a good few hours that was us all moved in.

I couldn't believe that we had an inside toilet, a bath and a wash hand basin in our bathroom, no more going downstairs to the stair head toilet and having to wait your turn. For the first time in my life we had soft toilet tissue paper and a verandah to stand on and look out at this South Nitshill. All of this I must say was a bit exciting, but the novelty would soon wear off and I yearned to be back home in the soo side. Over from us there had been four shops built but not occupied as of yet, so any shopping needing to be done was in the village of Nitshill, which was a fifteen minute walk away. They had a fish n chip shop, newsagents, barbers, butchers and greengrocers in the village and a Co-op shop (so at least ma still got her divvy) but it was a bit of a trek carrying all the shopping back to our new home, with mud and muck everywhere as half of the houses were still getting built.

One thing I noticed about Nitshill village was it had six pubs in it. The Househillwoood Tavern, The Royal Oak, The Cavendish, The Railway Inn, The Volunteers Arms and along a fair bit, the Nia roo, and in a few years time later I would have a drink in all of them. The Glasgow Corporation bus terminated here at Nitshill and the red SMT bus passed through here from Glasgow to a place called Neilston, which was a few miles further on. Instead of me walking to Holyrood School, I now had to catch two buses, that was the number forty eight going to Glasgow but I got off at Allison St in Govanhill and then a single decker bus going to Holyrood School.

My Granny Hendry still lived in the soo side and I would always go back to see her and it was a great feeling because this is where I felt that I belonged. In fact, some weekends I would stay overnight in my granny's single end and on Sunday travel back to South Nitshill. I would speak to all my pals and shopkeepers and they would ask me how I liked the new place. When I told them we had an inside toilet with soft toilet tissue paper and a verandah, they said "Oh you're so lucky" but secretly I would rather have stayed here in the soo side. If I could only have stayed here until I was twenty years old it would have meant oh so much more to me. I was still going to travel halfway round the world as a bricklayer, but I felt I was "robbed" of those seven years having to move away.

I looked at the Glue Pot Pub and Hurrels Bar and the Coronation Bar etc and I made myself a promise that when I was eighteen years old I would come back and have drink in all of them, just to be able to say later in years to come that I had done it before they were demolished.

I started to make new pals out in South Nitshill and of course we were all football mad. About half of my new pals were Rangers supporters and the rest, like me, supported Celtic, so we formed a wee football team and called ourselves 'Rancel' and played other local teams, and we weren't a bad side at all. I was thirteen years old by this time and at the weekend, well on a Friday night, I used to like going to the pictures, and I remember with all my new pals we went to see the film "The Magnificent Seven" in the Odeon picture house on Victoria Rd, just up from Eglinton Toll and it was brilliant. That's what we had to do if we wanted to see a film, get the bus into the toon, or like what I done normally and get off the bus at Eglinton St in the Gorbals and go to the Bedford Picture House or the Coliseum Picture House.

Later on in my life I would still be getting off at Eglinton Toll but it would be to go the Plaza Ballroom for dancing and a few drinks in the Star Bar and/or McNees Bar for a bit of 'Dutch courage' before trying to dance and chat up the ladies.

Then about six months after moving into our new home in South Nitshill, the number forty eight Glasgow Corporation bus that used to terminate at Nitshill, moved its terminus to more or less our close mouth. The shops opposite us had opened and I had a job as a milk boy delivering the early morning milk to the housing scheme where I now lived. There was a mobile chip shop which was actually a converted single decker bus, and it came round our housing scheme on a Friday night and it made a fortune, but the fish and chips were not a patch on the ones that Greasy Peter use to sell in the Gorbals. In addition, Frank Beltoushla who had a newsagents shop in the soo side and where I got my comics from, was now coming round our estate in a little van selling ice-cream, ginger, cigarettes and crisps etc.

I don't think there was a lot of planning went into these new housing estates on the outskirts of Glasgow. There was no play areas for the young weans, no football pitches, no community centres etc, it seemed that the houses were built as quick as possible and the people just dumped there. When we wanted to go to the dancing or the picture house we all had to get the bus into the toon and they could be packed, and you always seemed to get one of the drunks singing at the top of his voice and they always seemed to sit beside me!!

All of a sudden I'm in my last year at school and I'm almost fifteen years of age. My Granny Hendry was given a house in Nitshill, about a half hour's walk away from where we lived, and that was great company for my ma and I was always over in my granny's house. My trips back to the soo side were not as often now as they were when we first moved out to South Nitshill, but I did make the occasional trip and when I did the Gorbals clearance was really in full swing. The year now was 1963 and these multi stories seemed to be going up everywhere. I did go to Shawfield Stadium one Saturday to watch Clyde play my team Celtic and as I passed through Oatlands the regeneration plan there hadn't started yet.

My last day at school arrives and I'm feeling all excited. At dinner time I got the bus into the toon and went to Tam Shepherd's Joke Shop in Queen St and I buy stink bombs to let off in the classroom. When my last lesson started I judged the time to be about fifteen minutes to go 'til the final bell and I let the stink bombs drop. Oh what a smell, it was like rotten eggs and the teacher Mr McQueen said "Right who's done this?" and all my class mates pointed at me and said "It was Gill sir" so the teacher said "Right Gill, write out five hundred lines for Monday morning saying "I must not let off stink bombs in the classroom." I hope Mr McQueen never held his breath waiting for me to show up because when the last bell went I ran out of the school gate throwing all my school books up in the air and shouting out "I'm Free."

So that's me finished school, I'm fifteen years old and my ma takes me to the Career's Officer and he asks me what kind of work would I like and I answered straight away that I wanted to be a joiner (carpenter) as I always got top marks in the wood work class and I was always making shelves and other things in our house. This Career's Officer said "Oh I haven't got any vacancies for an apprentice joiner, but I have one for an apprentice bricklayer." I said "I don't want to be a brickie" then he said "The lad that I gave the joiner apprenticeship too will not make the grade, so you take the apprentice bricklayer's job, he will get the sack three months later and you'll get the apprentice joiners job. In fact, I will phone your mother when this happens." That happened 53 years ago and the phone never rang. What a blatant lie to tell a young fifteen year old lad, so I ended up a bricklayer for over forty six years, but I had a great life and my trade would take me to different countries, so no regrets from me.

I was told I would start work the following Monday with a Mr John Dickie and Sons so I told Dick the milkman the following morning that I wouldn't be his milk boy anymore and all he said when he gave me my ten shilling's wages for my seven days work was "Make sure you leave your milk bottle carriers in the milk crate." No good luck or thanks, his very last words were "I've got to look for another milk boy now."

So there am I standing at the corner of Saltmarket and Clyde St looking over the Albert Bridge into Crown St in the Gorbals and thinking how many times have I passed over the Albert Bridge before, but today is different as it is my first day at work. I got there about 7.00 am and waited as this was the pickup point for all the men who were working on the site that I was also going to. Some men started turning up, but being a fifteen year old boy just fresh from school, I was too shy to go over and introduce myself as the new apprentice. Anyway, John Dickie's van turns up and all the men pile into the back of it and as I go over to climb into the back of the van, the doors close and it drives away. I'm running after it shouting out "I'm the new apprentice" but it doesn't stop.

Oh what a disaster!! I'm left there standing in the middle of the road wondering what to do, so I get the bus back to South Nitshill and tell my ma what has happened, so she phones up John Dickie's office and tells Mr Dickie what has happened and he says that he had actually forgotten to tell the van driver that I was going to be there and said "Don't worry, tell Daniel (that's me) to come to our office and he can work in the joiners shop for his first day at work. Now disaster strikes for the second time that day as I am put with an old joiner whose every second word is a swear word, and it doesn't matter what piece of timber that I hand him when he asks for it, he just swears and says "That's no bloody good" and tells me that I am useless!!

Oh how I prayed for work to finish that day, and when it did, I ran out of that joiners shop like a greyhound and I made myself a promise there and then that in all of my life to come I would never be like that horrible person who I had to work with that day. Needless to say the following morning when I arrived at the pickup point for the van, I introduced myself to all the men there, as there was no way I was going back to that joiners shop and that horrible man, in fact I think I would rather have thrown myself into the River Clyde!!

Now as I write my book I am happy to say that I kept that promise and I always tried to be cheerful, and eventually later in life when I became foreman bricklayer, I always treated the men under my command with respect, and nine tens out of ten it worked. I had to sack a few people in my time but that's because they were liberty takers. I would always say to the men work with me, and not against me, and usually everything on site would be alright, after all it's hard enough coming to work so why not make it pleasant?

I must say in my five years apprenticeship with John Dickie, I was under the supervision of some great bricklayers, especially John Donlon (Senior) who was from Hospital St in the Gorbals. In fact, he was my mentor and made me into the bricklayer that I became. I'll never forget John and all the tricks of the trade that he showed me. There were a couple of men working for John Dickie who came from the Gorbals, there was John Donlon's son, young John Donlon and Ken McMasters, who both came from Thistle St and Jimmy Cairns who later would live in the new masionettes, just off of Caledonia Rd.

I was given a thoroughly good apprenticeship and was taught all aspects of my trade which later in life stood by me as I travelled halfway round the world to build bricks in other countries, but in all the sites that I worked on when serving my apprenticeship I never worked in the soo side. The nearest I came to working in the soo side was on an industrial estate beside Shawfield Stadium, a new factory being built in Maxwell Rd not far from Eglinton Toll and a few sites in Rutherglen.

I always remember when I was almost sixteen years old going to the Tradeston Tool Store in Eglinton st (opposite the Coliseum cinema) and asking for an American brick trowel called a Marshaltown trowel, and the sales assistant told me that because of the Vietnam war America need all their steel to make machine guns, and me, being a gullible young lad, fell for it. This assistant persuaded me to buy some other brick trowel but later that day when I went over into the toon, just at Glasgow Cross, there was another tool shop whose window was full of these Marshaltown trowels. I don't suppose I was the first young lad to be told a lie so as the shop assistant could make a sale, still we all live and learn!!

While working for John Dickie I met the love of my life, Rena Smith, who was a secretary in an office of a knitwear firm that we were refurbishing and we were together for eighteen months. In all my life Rena was the only girl I ever truly loved. We went to the movies during the week but at weekends on a Friday night we always went to the Clelland music lounge in Hospital St and the live music was fantastic. Of all the Gorbals pubs this had to be the best, and I think it was also the first pub to have live music in the soo side.

There was another pal of mine called Jimmy Curry who was a labourer for Dickie's and he lived on Pollokshaws Rd, just opposite the Granite City Pub (later to become 'The Brazen Head') and him and his wife lived in these new houses that had been allocated for the polis. They were nice two storey high houses with a wee verandah. Anyway, the Granite City pub was Jimmy's local and a good few times we would have a pint in there after work, then he would go home and I would make my way to Eglinton St to catch the 48 bus back home to South Nitshill.

Just at the corner of Cumberland St and Eglinton St under the railway bridge, you had the Kiloran Bar which was a nice wee pub. Right outside it was my bus stop and sometimes I would see my bus pass by just as I reached there, so I would pop into the Kiloran for a pint. There was usually a nice wee woman behind the bar and I would have a pint while trying to time the next bus back to Nitshill. Back in those days we didn't have all these smart phones that nowadays tell us the time when your next bus is due, you had to keep peeking out the door to see if your bus was coming and sometimes you had to leave half of your drink there as you saw your bus coming.

Another pub next door to the Kiloran was called the Office and the old joke was a man going home late would tell his wife he had to stay in the Office a bit late that night. One thing I do remember in the Office bar was it had a sign saying 'Foxes' outside the gents' toilet and 'Vixens' outside the ladies toilet. There were steps down to the gents' toilet and many a punter had a stumble, but that was a nice pub too.

One Friday night when I got my wage packet it had my wages at thirty hours of the fifth year apprentice bricklayers rate of pay, and the other ten hours at the bricklayers rate, so I phoned Dickie's office up and speak to Margaret, the wages clerk who tells me "Congratulations, your apprenticeship is over, you are now a tradesman." I said "Thank you, and now please take one weeks' notice as I shall be leaving the firm." I was always told by the seasoned bricklayers that you must never stay with the firm you have served your time with, otherwise you will always be treated as an apprentice.

I told all the men on the site that I was working on that my apprenticeship was over and the following Friday night I would be holding a farewell drink in the Star Bar at Eglinton Toll. I wanted to say goodbye to all the men that I had known for the previous five years. However, disaster was to strike, as on the following Monday morning, a friend of mine Charlie McDonald, a stonemason, asks me to give him a hand in shoving this scaffold tower which had castor wheels on the bottom of it. We gave it a good hard shove and a scaffold board from the top fell down and hit me on the base of my spine and knocked me out. I was taken to the hospital and given an x-ray, there was no spinal damage, just severe bruising, so I guess I was lucky.

I hobbled to Dickie's office that Friday and picked up my wages, and with everyone wishing me well, I made my way to the Star Bar for my farewell drink with all the men that I had worked with for the last five years, but no one showed up, they must have thought because of my injury I wouldn't turn up, now that was sad but nothing I could do about it, I just had a good drink in the Star Bar myself that night.

I stayed in Glasgow for about six months after finishing my apprenticeship, working on different sites. By this time my girlfriend Rena and I had parted company, but I honestly hope that she met a nice man and had a lovely family of her own, it's always your first love that you always remember. Now the time for me to start travelling had arrived and I left Glasgow to go to live and work in London, so with my suitcase, tool bag and level I left Glasgow Central Station with £15 and a fistful of dreams, never to return to see the soo side again for almost forty five years.

Chapter 7

So after an absence of forty four years and living and working in different countries, I now decide to go back and visit Oatlands and the Gorbals. When my parents were still alive I always went back to see them at least once a year, but with them living in Nitshill and Motherwell, I only ever passed through Glasgow city. Now that ma and da had passed away I kept promising myself that I would return to the street that I was brought up in, so many years ago, but kept putting it off as I had seen photos of the soo side on the internet and it just didn't look like the place where I had saw my formative years begin, and to be truthful, I also felt "awkward" and not sure of how I would feel.

The previous year I had been up in Glasgow when my nephew and his wife invited me up for a week's holiday, well not Glasgow as they live out in Airdrie, but I took a day trip into Glasgow to meet up with an old school pal from Wee Bonnies, Brian Donnelly. I had just started to learn how to use a computer and I went on one of the Facebook sites and got talking to Brian and he had agreed to meet me in Glasgow. We met up outside the Central Station and went for a few drinks and what a great old trip down memory lane we had. We had so much to talk about like old friends that we knew, and the soo side that we had been brought up in. Brian told me of all the changes that had taken place, but I really wanted to see it with my own eyes so to speak.

As I was staying out in Airdrie with my nephew, I decided to leave my visit to the soo side 'til the next year when I could book into a hotel in the city somewhere, and be only a bus ride away or a taxi ride away from the soo side, and have all of my holiday to spend in Glasgow, instead of worrying about getting a train back to Airdrie. In between this I found on Facebook a couple of sites "The Dampies," "Old Gorbals Pictures" and "Oatlands Memories." While on these sites I started speaking to "new friends" that I had found, and would you believe it, also a few old friends of mine that I had been brought up with in the soo side and some that I went to school with. Isn't this internet a great invention?

I told a few of my new and old friends that I was planning to come up to Glasgow the following year to visit the soo side and some of them said that they would meet up with me, in fact the first person who said she would meet me was Lynne Lees and I have never forgotten that. I was to become good friends with Lynne and her partner Garry Moore, and a rake of other Gorbals and Oatlands people, far too many to mention, but I will just say Eddie Graham, Carol Connolly, Peter Mortimer, Lorraine White plus so many more. I must say that waiting for my holiday the following year seemed to take forever, it was great being able to speak to people on the Facebook sites every day and there were photos being shown that I never thought I would ever see again in my lifetime.

There was actually a school class photo of me aged five years old in Wee Bonnies school. Brian Donnelly had posted this for me and I recognised half of the boys and girls straight away, oh boy, never in my wildest dreams did I ever think I would have an old school photo from my past and later on in a few years time I would meet up with five of them.

Then the time finally arrived and it was time for me to go back to Glasgow. I booked into the Travelodge Hotel in the city in Hill St, just round the corner from Sauchiehall St, this was a nice clean hotel. It used to be years ago that when I lived in a hotel they would give you a room key but you had to leave it at the desk when you went out, but nowadays with all this modern technology they held you a piece of plastic and this opened your door and you kept it with you when you went out.

I landed on the Wednesday and my meeting up with my new friends was to be in the Brazen Head Pub (formerly the Granite City, where I once drank with my pal Jimmy Curry), on the coming Friday night. First thing I did the next morning was to buy a weekly bus pass to get me about and this seven day pass cost £14 which seemed reasonable to me, but what shocked me was all the numbers of the buses and routes had changed since I had lived in Glasgow forty five years earlier!!

What I did was get a bus that I thought would go to the Gorbals, but it tuned into George Square. I got off the bus feeling like an eejit and walked down Queen St until I came to Lewis's building in Argyle St, but it wasn't called Lewis's anymore, it was part Debenhams and other shops, and the Argyle St where I used to catch an old shoogly tram was half-pedestrianised, oh it sure had changed. So I walked along to the Trongate 'til I came to Saltmarket, passing by where once Paddy's market had been and over the Albert Bridge to Crown St, but wait a minute, this is not Crown St, it can't be I thought to myself. I felt like I was in a different city.

I turned left along Ballater St and knew if I kept walking then I must come to McNeil St where I used to go to the library when I was a wean. I'm walking along Ballater St and the tenements have all gone and for me it feels unreal, then eventually I come to McNeil St and I think "Thank God it's still here." I pass by the Pig and Whistle pub which I remember all those years ago, although it's now only a single story with no building above it. I somehow cut through the side streets and find myself facing the Southern Necropolis Graveyard and I think well at least I can get my bearings from here and as I turn left and walk down Caledonia Rd, I see St Bonaventure's Church is gone as is the Ritz Picture House and the Coronation Bar and it all looks and feels surreal.

Then I spot the Hutchensontown Bowling Green and its club house, but next to the bowling green where you once had the "sony pon" in Richmond Park, that had gone too and they were building flats on it. I couldn't believe that houses were being built in Richmond Park!! Then with my back against the Bowling Green's railings and wee wall (which was as I remembered it all those years ago) I looked over to where my street Fauldhouse St was. I looked and it was no longer called Fauldhouse St but Fauldhouse Way, so at least they had kept the name but the steamie had gone and so had Big Bonnies school. I have only cried a few times in my life (when ma and da had passed away) but that morning I had tears in my eyes as I thought back to the days of me being a wean, when the tenements were still standing, when my parents, sister and granny and granda and friends were still alive and I had a lump in my throat as big as a football.

I had brought a digital camera with me but I just didn't feel like taking any photos that day. I walked away feeling very remorseful and walked back to McNeil St and went to the Pig and Whistle pub which was open and went in for a drink. I got speaking to the girl who ran the pub, her name was Flo, and she made me very welcome, and after telling her I was on a visit back to the auld place, she said to everyone in the bar "Hey guys, here's a man who has returned to his roots after being away from the soo side for forty five years" and I got speaking to a lot of the customers, and nice people they were too. One nice touch about this pub was it had black and white photos all over the walls of the way Oatlands and the Gorbals was in the days of the tenements. After having a good drink in the Pig and Whistle I was told by the customers that there was a wee single decker bus that passed along Ballater St on the half hour and hour that would take me back into the toon, so I caught this bus and then walked along to Hope St and caught a bus that I thought would take me up to Sauchiehall St and my hotel, but it turned right into the George Square direction and I thought I'm back in my home town but I just haven't a clue where the bloomin' buses are going, so much has changed since I've been away.

Then I go back to my Travelodge Hotel that afternoon and have a siesta. I used to think when I was a wean it was funny how my granny or granda would have a wee sleep in the afternoon or just doze in their chair, but now I'm sixty eight years old I find that I'm doing the same myself, especially since I retired from work seven years ago and am up half the night going to the toilet, then reading a book and perhaps not going to sleep till about 5.00 am. I think it's called the ageing process (ha ha).

Come the Friday morning I spot a bus, a number 57 and it has South Nitshill as its destination and I think "Yes, I want to go and see what Nitshill looks like now just for my peace of mind," so although I have arthritis in my knees, hands and foot, I climb up the stairs of the bus to get a grandstand view of everything as we pass by. We go up Bridge St and it looks more or less the same with a few tenement buildings still standing but they look run down and dilapidated. I see the Laurieston Bar and think I must pop in there for a pint one day while I'm up in Glasgow on my holidays, then along Eglinton St the Kiloran Bar is still there, but closed down and to the left there seems to be some big motorway, where once stood lovely looking tenements designed by the "Greek " Architect, Alexander Thomson. We then come to the Star Bar where I should have held my party when I had finished my apprenticeship, and I think to myself that I must pop in there too and have a pint and a look round.

I look over from the Star Bar to where McNees Pub and the Plaza Ballroom used to stand and they are no longer there and I think back to when I was a young man on a Friday or Saturday night going into the Star Bar or McNees to have a bit of "Dutch courage" before going into the Plaza for some dancing, and maybe, if I was lucky, to get a lumber and take the girl home and make a date for the following night but this seems so long ago in the past now.

Then the bus that I'm on passes by Allison St where I used to catch the single decker bus to my old school, Holyrood and then we pass Queens Park, which I only ever was in a couple of times and then we arrive at Shawlands Cross. Now Shawlands, although only ten minutes away on the bus from the Gorbals, was always known as an upmarket area with fine tenement buildings and oh so many different shops and a few pubs. The pub I remember at Shawlands Cross (where Kilmarnock Rd and Pollokshaws Rd meet) used to be called 'Samuel Dows' and it was a great meeting place with it being at that intersection. People would meet and have a drink while doing their shopping but " Sammy Dow's " is no longer there, it has been replaced by one of these Bistro bars and I think another piece of history has gone.

My bus travels on but it doesn't turn right the way it used to do, it turns left into Thornliebank and passes by Burnfield Rd where the offices of my former employer, John Dickie and Sons used to be and I think that I must go there one day and look at the offices, just for old times' sake.

Now the bus turns into the Carnwadric and Arden areas and I must admit that I am totally lost and wonder if indeed this bus is going to South Nitshill? Well, after twenty minutes or so we come upon the housing scheme of South Nitshill where we moved to after the back of our tenement had collapsed in the soo side. What a shock!! It looks like the housing scheme that I knew all those years ago has disappeared to be replaced with new private houses. All the buildings that I had delivered milk to when I was a milk boy, over more than half a century ago have gone and I just can't believe it.!!

Next the bus takes another diversion and I find myself back down in the valley area of South Nitshill where ma and da had our house so many years ago, and lo and behold it's still there. As I pass by it on the bus I look at the wee verandah and there is somebody standing there and I feel like shouting out "Hey I used to live there." We then arrive in the village of Nitshill itself and all the pubs that I drank in so many years ago have all gone except one. That pub was called 'The Cavendish' but now it has changed its name to 'The Hazelwood.' The fish and chip shop is still there as is the bookmakers and the newsagents.

I got off the bus and had a walk around looking at all that surrounded me, and most of what had been there when I was a young man has completely gone. Although I never really took to living in Nitshill, it still comes as a bit of a shock, so I stood there in the rain (yes it was raining, ah well some things never change), having a good look round, and then I boarded a bus back to Glasgow city again. I know that I will never see Nitshill again in my lifetime, but I just wanted for my own peace of mind to see it for the last time.

That same night was the night I was meeting up with some of my new friends in the Brazen Head Pub in the Gorbals and I was feeling all excited that people had said they would turn up and meet me. I think there was actually nine girls that turned up that night, Carol Connelly, Carol Grant, Lynne Lees, Mags McFadden, Josie Stuksis, Lorraine White, Barbara Carroll, Donna Harley and Angie and I felt very humbled that all these lovely ladies had went out of their way to meet up with me, and what a terrific night we all had. We were reminiscing about times gone by, although I must say I was the oldest person there with the girls being a lot younger than me. Yes, this was a great welcome home to me and I will never forget it. Oh yes, and we had a few drinks too!!

Saturday, the following day, was another special day for me too as I was meeting up with some friends in the Laurieston Bar in Bridge St where the Gorbals ends and the Kinning Park area of Glasgow begins. Actually the owners of the Laurieston Bar are the Clancy family and what nice people they are, always making you feel welcome when you walk into their pub, in fact, they had lived in the soo side at number 63 Wolseley St (right opposite the "hoat wa' of the steamie that I had mentioned earlier) when I lived in Fauldhouse St, although I only vaguely remember them.

I went into the lounge bar of the Laurieston Pub and was met once more by Brian Donnelly my old school classmate, Paddy Cawley, and his lovely wife. Paddy I had met on one of the Gorbals Facebook sites and I had shared a laugh or two with him. Then later on another old school classmate of mine came in, it was Geana Sweeney (McPike now), who had so wonderfully sang Elvis Presley's "All shook up" at our school Christmas party and her friend Jean Mullen, who had also lived in Oatlands. Well what a great fabulous day we all had and once again we talked about our lives way back in the days when the tenements were still standing, and what we had all done with our lives and what children we now had, a truly great get together and once again, I felt very pleased that people would take the time and come and meet me.

On a few days of my holiday I had a good walk through the Gorbals and was trying to find my way because for me after being away for forty five years it looked all so "strange." On my way up on the train from London I had thought, in my naivety, that I would walk into the Clelland Bar in Hospital St and have a drink in there. I thought how I would tell the barman how I had used the pub way back in the late nineteen sixties and how I had loved going into the music lounge with my girlfriend Rena on Friday nights when the lounge bar was packed to the gunnels, and everyone singing along with the band to the hits of the day, whether it was "Delilah" by Tom Jones or "Please Release Me Let Me Go" by Engelbert Humperdink, but when I got to where the Clelland used to stand it, was no longer there and another part of me "died."

In fact, when I went to look for Gorbals Cross it just was no longer there. I found this so hard to try and comprehend. I know people that had stayed in the greater Gorbals area all their lives and never moved to the housing schemes or further afield would not have noticed the changes so much as me because it happened a bit at a time to them but to me who had been gone for forty five years, it was a complete bombshell and I just couldn't believe it. I had a few drinks in the Laurieston Bar before I went back to London and had a good old talk with John Clancy. During the daytime and some nights, I would go in there and have a talk with his brother James, who did the evening shifts behind the bar. They are two great characters and the stories came flying thick and fast over their years in the pub trade. Then again, us Glaswegians have always been noted for our friendliness and it's not something that I forget, it's just that living in the London area, if you try and start up a conversation with someone in a public house, it makes you think "What are they after" and alarm bells start to ring. Oh it was really good to have met up with old friends and my new friends too, but it would take me a few more holidays back home in Glasgow to try and find my "bearings."

I had a walk about the toon, and it seems the streets are all still there, but the shops all seemed to have changed. One particular example of this is "Dizzy Corner" which was where Boots the Chemist used to be at the corner of Agyle Street and Union Street, (where KFC (Kentucky Fried Chicken) is now). Well, "Dizzy Corner" was a popular meeting place for couples meeting to go out on a date and you would wait for your date hoping that she would turn up. I was let down a few times myself.

All of a sudden I only have one day left of my holiday back home in Glasgow and the old arthritis in my knees starts to play up. I was going to go to the Star Bar at Eglinton Toll and visit Burnfield Rd in Thornliebank where the offices of John Dickie and Sons where, and even though I had heard through the building trade grapevine that John Dickie and Sons had been taken over by another building firm, I still wanted to go and have a look at the offices that I helped to build when I was a sixteen year old 2nd year apprentice bricklayer, but would now leave this to the following year, if God spared me.

So the next day arrives and I walk down Hope St to the Central Railway Station after checking out of my Travelodge hotel. As I sit on one of the seats waiting for my trains departure platform notification, I think back to all those years ago in 1968 when I stood here, in the same railway station, just starting out on my life's adventures and smile to myself. It sure has been a great adventure for me with lots of ups and downs along the way, but then again, I wouldn't have had it any other way.

Now I'm sitting in the Virgin train that is taking me back to London town and we pull out of the Central Station. It's always great when you're on your way home, but it's a bit of a downer when you are leaving, but in another years time I will be coming back again. These trains nowadays only take four and a half hours from Glasgow to London, but when I was travelling in my younger days it was eight hours, and sometimes even longer, with no buffet car or heating like we have nowadays.

Right, now I'm back in London and living in my wee sheltered housing flat again and start putting by money each week from my state pension for my next visit back to Glasgow. I'm in daily contact via Facebook with all my pals in the soo side and there are a few photos posted of all the people that I met up with plus myself on the day or night of that event which pleases me no end. Then there is talk of a Gorbals Reunion bash to be held in the Glencairn Club (just past Shawfield Stadium and on the road to Rutherglen) and this will be the very first Gorbals reunion ever held, so I said to myself "Oh yes, that's for me, and I would plan my next year's holiday round that date.

A friend of mine, Margaret McGuigan Bonner, said she would get me a ticket and give it to me on the night at the Glencairn Club and I would pay her when I saw her. Well I couldn't wait and the countdown was then on, not only for me but for everyone else who was going to attend the reunion and all the money gathered that night would go to the Prince and Princess of Wales hospice based in the Gorbals.

After all the waiting, the time arrives for me to return to Glasgow on my yearly holiday. I have bought my ticket online from Virgin trains and also this year instead of going to the Travelodge Hotel in Hill St I book into the Eurostar Hostel on the corner of Jamaica St and Clyde St and only a few minutes' walk from the Gorbals, and it's almost half the price of the Travelodge. The only drawback being, instead of me having a double bed as I did with Travelodge, here in the Eurostar it's a metal framed bunk bed and you have to make your own bed each morning (well sure I do that every morning in my flat in London so there's no problem there). Obviously this is a single room for me as I won't share with anyone. I think the reason the Eurostar Hostel is so cheap is that it has many rooms with ten or so bunk beds in large dormitory rooms for people who are sharing in groups and back packers who are looking for the cheapest stay.

I travel up in the Virgin train and it's great to be able to have a cup of coffee or cup of tea and sandwich (or a beer) from the buffet car, sit and relax and before you know where you are, we are drawing into Glasgow Central Station and as always when arriving back in Glasgow I put my feet onto the platform and I feel the "electric charge" running up my legs and I feel like shouting out "I'm hame!!" So I walk the short distance down Union St past "Dizzy Corner" down Jamaica St and check into the Eurostar Hostel. I unpack my wee suitcase, have a quick wash to freshen up and as the time is six o'clock in the evening, I walk the short distance over the Glasgow Bridge spanning the River Clyde along Bridge St and walk into the Laurieston Bar and meet up with Davie Scott from Moffat St. This is the first time Davie and myself have met face to face, we had been talking to each other on Facebook for ages, but this was our first meeting and what a great night we had. Having a few "swallys" and catching up with all that was happening in the soo side.

John Clancy and his son Joe were serving us from behind the bar and we had a good old talk with them too. One of the things I like about the Laurieston Bar is you always get a pre-chilled pint glass from a fridge, it seems to make the lager taste better, and they have hot pie and peas on sale if you fancy a snack. This is the snack food I remember a lot of the pubs in Glasgow used to have before I left in the late sixties. Another Facebook friend from one of the Gorbals sites is in the pub too, Eamon O'Donnell and we have a good old talk with Eamon too. When its ten o'clock I say cheerio to Davie and I make my way back to the Eurostar Hostel for a good night's sleep.

First thing in the morning, I wake up have a shower as the rooms are en suite, make my bed and head over Jamaica St to Wetherspoon's pub and order two rolls on square sausage. If there's one food I miss from being away from Glasgow, then it's the Lorne sausage and I always smother it in brown sauce, oh it tastes great. Then I make my way to the Brazen Head pub where Lynne Lees works as the cleaner, and as she just finishes her shift we sit down and have a drink, a pint for me and a glass of lemonade for her. Lynne's partner, Garry Moore then comes in, bringing their two dogs 'Columbo' and 'Spot' and we have a great old talk and I tell them how much that the soo side has changed since I left it.

I remember when this pub was called the Granite City and I used to have a drink in it with my old work mate, Jimmy Curry. In fact one night way back in the late sixties, I ordered a pint of Guinness, took a quick sip and went to the toilet. When I came back my pint had filled back up again!! This was because there were water drips coming down from the ceiling (as there was the railway bridge over it and water seeped into the pubs roof) and where my pint was standing on the bar was right underneath the drips coming down. After a few drinks I left and took a walk along Cumberland St, but it all so different to me. The tenements had all gone, but the one building that hadn't been demolished was St Francis' Church, it was now the John Mains Centre (named after a former politician who's Ward was this part of the Gorbals many years previously) but I clearly remember in my mind's eye the Cumberland St that I used to know, with all its shops and people busily hurrying about, and there always seemed a buzz to the street, but now as I looked at it, it seemed almost empty and forlorn.

The following day on the Saturday I got the bus down to the Star Bar at Eglinton Toll and when I walked in there it was just the way that I remembered it, almost nothing had changed. It seems that they do a great lunch in the lounge bar and pretty cheap too. I had a pint of lager and told the barman that years ago I had drunk in there when the manager's name was 'Dougie,' but he was only a young lad, so he wouldn't have remembered him, which reminded me that I was not the young man I used to be when I last frequented the Star Bar.

I had bought another weekly bus pass this year when I came home and I was slowly getting to know what buses went where, so I decided to go and visit Burnfield Rd where John Dickie's offices and joiners workshop was. I caught the correct bus from Eglinton Toll and got off at Burnfield Rd. While walking along Burnfield Road I thought to myself "How many times had I walked this same road in my apprenticeship years?" There still stood on one side the houses that I had known, but on the other side there was a factory and other buildings that hadn't been there years ago. I then came to where John Dickie's offices and workshop had been, but it was gone!!

There was nothing there. They had been bulldozed. There was just a large piece of barren wasteland and it shocked me. I must say, the only thing that remained was a brick pillar gate post that my mentor John Donlon had built. I remembered watching him build it in 1964 and as I stood there looking at it now, a cold shiver ran down my back. I then caught a bus back to Jamaica St and went into the Imperial Bar in Howard St, just round the corner from the Eurostar Hostel, and had a good drink to try and drown my sorrows.

I had been talking to Colin Mackie on Facebook for a while, Colin came from Oatlands in the era of when the tenements were still standing and it was he who started up the "Oatlands Memories" Facebook site where people can post photos and talk about the old times (and the present day times too). Colin is a very down to earth lovely nice man who is also Chairman of the Southern Necropolis Action Group, which looks after the upkeep of the Southern Necropolis Graveyard on Caledonia Rd in the Gorbals, and this is among many other activities that Colin is involved with. Anyway, the following day which was Sunday, I met up with Colin and his fiancée, Elsie (now his beautiful wife) in the Southern Necropolis Graveyard and we had a good old walk round looking at the headstones that had been there for so many years and Colin told me of all the work that the volunteer workers do to keep the graveyard clean and tidy.

In addition, there are many people from home and abroad who want to find out where the graves of their ancestors are situated, and Colin does his best to try and locate them. All this, and the cutting of the ivy from around the headstones is taken care of by Colin and Rick Hart (just to name a couple) and so many other people which is tremendous work. In my eye they are all truly unsung heroes and that is just one reason that I donated all the royalty payments of my last book "Gorbals and Oatlands" to go towards the upkeep of the graveyard. It seems so strange looking back now, but it's here that I used to play with my pals when we were just weans, sixty years earlier.

We had a good old talk and walk round the graveyard for two hours even though it was raining (umbrellas to the rescue) and it was great to have met up with Colin and Elsie and be given a guided tour of the Southern Necropolis, many thanks again to them both.

Now the Gorbals Reunion bash at the Glencairn Club on the Friday is getting closer and on the Thursday night I had agreed to meet some people in Sharkey's pub, just close to Ballater St. I had to meet up with Norah Greene, Lorraine White, her daughter Laura and fiancé, Graeme, and we did, and we had a great night. A few drinks and a few memories were shared of times gone by. I had also said that I would meet up with Ann Ward and members of her family, some of them having flown in from Jersey in the Channel islands for the reunion, so that was more memories to share. Ann and her family had originally come from Hospital St and she can clearly remember skating on the smooth surface of Hospital St just beside the Clelland bar. Oh yes, all in all we all had a terrific night in Sharkey's bar and when the night was over Angie Best (nee Peden) another new friend of mine, phoned for a taxi for me (thanks Angie).

Now the big night had arrived. I went to the Laurieston Bar and had a beer and then asked Joe Clancy behind the bar to phone me a taxi to take me to the Glencairn Club. I went there early as I was donating two copies of my book "Have Trowel Will Travel" to be raffled on the night with the money going towards the Prince and Princess of Wales Hospice. Now, Christina Gray, who had done such a wonderful job of organising the reunion had a chair and a table ready for me, just beside the front door, where people could see my book and buy a few raffle tickets but it wasn't only me that was selling raffle tickets, oh no, there were quite a few people involved in this and fair play to them all.

Gerry Gracie another one of my new friends did such a marvellous job of walking round all the tables selling raffle tickets for all the great prizes that people had kindly donated on the night. In fact, the money collected on the night of the very first Gorbals

Reunion night was over £2,000, which was absolutely tremendous. I have to say that the Glencairn was jam packed that night. I sat at my wee table 'til 9.30 pm that night then all the money I had collected for my books I handed to one of the lovely girls sitting at the table where all the other raffle prizes were on show. I also handed over the two copies of my book which I had personally signed for the winners and then I sat down and had a drink with my pals, Davie Scott and Seonaid Delmore and enjoyed listening to the music. It really was a great night and the ladies all looked fantastic. The icing on the cake was when Saint Francis Pipe Band came marching into the hall playing on the bagpipes "Oh When The Saints Go Marching In" but what lifted the roof was when they played "Scotland the Brave." Such a cheer went up, it sounded like the 'Hampden roar' after Scotland had scored the winning goal. What a great night and it was great talking to so many people like Lynne Lees and her partner Garry Moore, my wee pal Alex King, and fair play to Angelina Best (nee Peden) for taking our photos. What a great night to remember.

The following day on the Saturday I had arranged to meet up with my primary school pal, Billy Harvie, who I hadn't seen in over fifty years since I left the soo side after our tenement building had collapsed. I had earlier that year saw a comment on Facebook about 'Wee Bonnie's football teams' and Billy had left a comment, and before I knew it, me and Billy were talking again after all those years. We met up in the Laurieston lounge bar, Billy came along with his lovely wife Liz and what a great catch up we had. Can you imagine what stories we had to swap about what had happened in our lives? The children and grandchildren that we both had, what our work lives had been like etc? All this is thanks to Facebook and the internet. I had never in my wildest dreams thought that I would have seen my pal Billy again.

On the same day in the Laurieston Bar, another old friend of mine, Oni Hayes from Hamilton came in to see me and Roberta Gaffney and her husband Charlie. We really did have a great afternoon and as I had mentioned previously, the 'sub-crawl' people would come into the pub for one or two quick drinks (for charity), the pub would be packed for half an hour, then they would go, get on the subway for the next pub on their list and our company would be on our own again. It all added up to a great atmosphere that day. Later on that day Eddie Graham and his wife Brenda came in. Eddie is a great Gorbals character and very knowledgeable into the bargain too. I had met Eddie the previous night at the Gorbals Reunion after speaking to him on Facebook for ages and the latest project that Eddie was involved in was the Restoration of the Albert Bridge, which is the bridge that cross from Crown St in the Gorbals over to the Saltmarket, on the other side of the River Clyde.

I left the Laurieston Pub at eight o'clock that night and what a day I had. It really was great meeting up with my friends that day. I went back to my Euro Hostel that evening and had a good sleep. I think all the drinking that I had done since I had arrived in Glasgow had just about caught up with me. When I was working as a bricklayer I used to have about five or six pints every night after work, but now since I have retired I only ever go out to the pub once in a blue moon, as the state pension that I receive doesn't go that far, but I'm not complaining as I can save up for my yearly holiday back to Glasgow, have enough money for all my families birthday presents etc and have enough left for my food each week.

My last days of my holidays are here and I walk over the road to the Wetherspoon's Bar (which has pretty cheap prices) and just have a few beers to calm me down. I buy a copy of the Sunday Post newspaper and just relax for the day. Then all of a sudden it's time to go back to London and as I have said before, it's great arriving in Glasgow but definitely a downer going back. So I land back in London, back once more in my wee flat and start saving up for my holiday next year, altogether it really has been a fabulous time meeting up with friends old and new.

Chapter 8

Now when I'm back in London I always meet up with a pal of mine, Gary Thomson (also a member of 'Old Gorbals Pictures' Facebook site) twice a year for a drink, and I catch with all the news. Gary left the Gorbals and moved out to Toryglen with his parents, but like me, he now lives in London, well actually a place called Morden which is at the beginning of Surrey. We always meet up in a Wetherspoon's Pub as the prices are very reasonable. It's good to sit face to face and have a talk and a laugh about back home and what happened a few years back.

I'm also on another couple of Facebook sites that cover the Greater Glasgow area like 'Glescapals' and 'Glasgow Banter,' in fact, over the last few years that I have visited Glasgow on my holidays, I have met up with some of the 'Glasgow Banter' members and we've all sat down and had a great old time. First time I met up with the banters group we met up in St Enoch's Square in a pub called 'The Hootenanny.' It's good to put faces to names that you usually only talk to on Facbook. They're all from different areas in Glasgow with everyone thinking their area is the best (when we all know it's the soo side) (ha ha). This is a yearly meet up for us now and once again the toon is a central meeting point for us all.

On the topic of St Enoch's Square, it seems like only yesterday when I used to go to the railway station there and do my train spotting, but I'm afraid that the St Enoch's Square that I knew in my younger days has changed completely. I remember that the corporation buses used to have their terminus there and B.O.A.C (British Overseas Aircraft Company which later amalgamated with B.E.A. British European Airways to form what we know today as British Airways) had a great big office and the subway station was that wee red sandstone building that looks like a miniature castle. I will never ever forget that "smell" as you walked down into the subway and I'm sure other Glaswegians will never forget that smell too.

I look around and I have to pinch myself because in the place of the old St Enoch's Railway Station is this massive glass roofed multi shopping centre with so many shops and it seems that there are escalators everywhere, which is good as my old legs play me up terrible if I have to climb stairs. What a place it is inside. There are so many places you can sit down and have something to eat. Then I look along Howard St to where I used to use a pub called the "Old Eagle Inn" where I had tried my first pint of German beer many years ago when I was a young man. I know you must expect changes to happen, but somewhere in the back of your mind you still expect it to be the same as it was before you left your native city.

It's like now when I go to the old Lewis's building and I think back to when I went there with my ma to queue up for Santa's Grotto, then later to buy airfix model aeroplane kits, or as a fifteen year old going downstairs to the basement for the music department and squeezing into one of the music booths with your pals to listen to a record before you bought it. It always sticks in my mind that way back in the mid nineteen sixties you could buy a single record for 6/8d old money, or, if you had the money, you could buy three single records for exactly £1.

Memories like this have stayed with me all of my life, but now when I look at Lewis's it's not Lewis's anymore, and another part of my life seems to have disappeared

Anyway there is talk of an Oatlands Reunion bash to be held in the Glencairn Club on the 29th August and it's being organised by my good friend, Colin Mackie, and his good wife Elsie, (yes they have married since the last time I saw them) with all the proceeds going towards the West of Scotland Deaf Society and also Oatlands Children which is terrific. I order three tickets, one each for my school pal Billy Harvie, his lovely wife Liz, and myself, and that is another great event to look forward to and I might just meet up with a few old friends from years ago when I lived in Fauldhouse St.

In between going up to Glasgow on my yearly holiday I wrote another book called "Gorbals and Oatlands" and I donated all the proceeds from the book to go towards the upkeep of the Southern

Necropolis Graveyard on Caledonia Rd in the Gorbals. It consisted of 70 of my short poems, a compilation of different peoples stories about growing up in the area and songs we sang in the streets of the soo side when we were growing up as weans, and a few photos. This was my way of putting something back into the soo side and saying thank you for my wonderful childhood and growing up there.

On that point, I must thank Martha Brindley very much for recommending the publisher to me (as Martha had written the life story of her brother Iain McColl the TV star of many shows (RIP) as the publisher that I wrote my autobiography with was so expensive. This new publisher was very reasonable with his price and Martha helped me along greatly with questions that I had, and made life a lot easier for me, many thanks to you Martha.

I'm still in daily contact with all my pals on Facebook but I have to say although the internet is brilliant, I found myself joining too many Facebook sites and to be truthful, it was starting to take over my life, so I cut myself down to just four groups with Old Gorbals Pictures and Oatlands Memories being the main two. I'm sure that many people who are on Facebook will know what I mean.

The time arrives and I have bought my train ticket online from Virgin trains and booked once more back into the Euro Hostel in Jamaica St. Once again, because I have booked early for the hostel, I get a really good deal. I find myself sitting on the Virgin train from Euston Station in London and sitting having a coffee and sandwich and thinking it won't be long now 'til I land back in Glasgow. My train is half an hour late in arriving in Central Station but that's no problem, sure it has only taken five hours, and as I step onto the platform that electric charge runs up my legs again, and I'm back home in my native city, and I think 'magic.'

Once again I head to the Euro Hostel, have a quick wash and head over the Glasgow Bridge along Bridge St, and into the Laurieston Bar. I order a pint of Guinness and James Clancy (one of the owners of the bar) comes and sits down beside me and we have a great old talk. It really is such a friendly pub and I get speaking to a few men who are sitting across from me and the night just flew in. As I said before, Glaswegians are really friendly people. Then all of a sudden it's 10.00 pm and this Thursday has absolutely flown in. I bid James Clancy and the bar good night and I walk back to the Euro Hostel and I am soon in the land of nod.

Next morning, Friday, I am up early and shower and shave, then it's over to Wetherspoon's Pub and have the full Scottish breakfast. It's brilliant. Egg, bacon, black pudding. square sausage, tottie scone and a mug of tea. I have a walk about the toon as it's only 9.00 am. I take a walk up to where 'Dizzy Corner' used to be and just laugh into myself, then I walk along Argyle St, up Queen St and into George Square and you know the square hasn't really changed at all over the years. Walking back down Queen St I pass by Tam Shepard's joke shop and think back to when it was my last day at school and I bought those stink bombs.

I go into Lidl's Supermarket and I always buy some chocolates for Lynne Lees and the barmaids in the Brazen Head Pub and as it's half an hour to go 'til the pubs open, I take a slow leisurely walk along Clyde St then over the suspension bridge (how many times did I cross this when I was a wean?) I have just timed it right as it's eleven o'clock and the Brazen Head Pub is just opening its doors and I walk in and give Lynne a hug and say hello to the bar staff.

Then Garry Moore, Lynne's partner walks in with the two dug's, Columbo and Spot and we sit down and catch up with all the news and have a great old time. I have arranged to meet up with a few people this day so I have a couple of pints of lager to get me into the swing of things.

At 1.00 pm that afternoon my Facebook friend, Paul Hart, walked into the pub, this is the first time we have met and we sit down to have a great old blether. Paul is a good bit younger than me (by 18 years) and Paul would have been born when the Gorbals clearance was in full swing, and the multi story flats were sprouting up, and the old tenements of my era were vanishing, yes changes were happening big time when he was born in 1966. In fact, this very pub the Brazen Head that we were having a drink in today was called the Granite City back then, and as I previously mentioned, I had drank in there in the late nineteen sixties.

Anyway, another friend of mine called Oni Hayes, who now lives out in Hamilton also came into the pub to meet me and between the three of us a good drinking session ensued. We were also having a talk with some of the regular drinkers who used the Brazen Head as their local. Then Carol Connolly, her sister Sandra and friend Lorraine McIvor all came into the pub to join my company and what a great laugh we all had. Carol, Sandra and Lorraine have a Facebook page called "3 Gorbals Girls Out and About with Friends" and are always posting photos when they are out. Then Maria Coyle joined our company and as we were having a good drink everybody was telling their different stories of what they got up to in the past when the tenements were still standing, and even after that when the new buildings took over.

I know that I have said it before, but soo side people and Glaswegians in general are friendly people, and we like nothing better than to sit down, have a drink and listen to each other's yarns, while of course telling our own yarns. By this time I was getting a bit bloated with the beer I had drank so I decided to go on the vodka and coke. Everyone else seemed to be drinking vodka or wine or whisky and this seemed to make everyone's stories seem all the better (funnier). The time was flying in and Janice the barmaid had to keep coming over to our table to take away all the empty glasses, we were all having a ball.

I had met Carol on a few occasions before when I had visited Glasgow and a real down to earth girl she is too, but this was the first time that I had met her sister, Sandra, and her friend, Lorraine, but it was like we had all know each other for years. My old friend Brian Donnelly from my primary school days also popped in that night when he had finished work and that made our company even better, although I must say with Brian being sober after just finishing work, he was sitting among us who had been drinking for over five hours and I know that when this happens it's like people are on different wave lengths, but fair play to Brian, he stayed for an hour and a couple of pints before catching the bus back home for his evening meal.

I thanked Brian for taking the time to come and see me after he had finished work, also Maria who left just after Brian. Then with the time nearing 7.30 pm, Paul Hart decided to leave. Fair play to Paul for coming to meet up with me too (especially as Paul has breathing problems and has to carry a small oxygen bottle with him everywhere he goes). That left Carol, Sandra, Lorraine, Oni and myself and we had another few drinks for the road and left the Brazen Head at 9.00 pm, but what a great day we all had, and I must thank everyone who had taken the time to come and meet up with me that day.

The following day was the Oatlands Reunion bash out at the Glencairn Club which starts at 7.30 pm in the evening so I don't want to start drinking in the morning or afternoon as I would be "steaming" when the evening came, but I really had a hangover from yesterday's session in the Brazen Head, so I went over the road to the Wetherspoon's pub in Jamaica St and had pint of cider and a full Scottish breakfast which was marvellous.

Killing time I went for a walk about the toon and went to Buchanan St and the House of Fraser, what a really big store this is and I must have been in there for well over an hour and then I paid a wee visit to the Argyle Arcade, and all those jewelers shops with all those diamonds and Rolex watches.

Next I found myself in Renfield St and standing outside the Odeon cinema, memories of taking my girlfriend Rena to the pictures every Wednesday night here came flooding back, and one night especially stands out in my mind. We had gone to see the film "Swiss Family Robinson" starring John Mills. Anyway, we walked into the cinema foyer and I went to the ticket window and bought our tickets, I then turned round and took Rena by the elbow to lead her into the cinema hall but Rena was standing in front of me!! When I looked, I was holding the arm of another girl by mistake, I apologised straight away but the look on Rena's face was something to behold. Well if looks could have killed then I would have been dead straight away. Needless to say there was no back seat winching that night!!

Then I took a slow walk back to my Euro Hostel and lay on top of my bed and had an afternoon siesta but making sure that I had set the alarm on my Smart phone for 5.00 pm in the evening as I had the Oatlands Reunion bash to go to. I got up from my bed at 5.00 pm and had a shower and shave and got dressed up. I walked over the Glasgow Bridge spanning the River Clyde then onto Bridge St and into the Laurieston Bar where I had a pint of beer and hot pie and peas to give me something in my stomach to soak up the beer when attending the reunion bash later.

I met Eamon O'Donnell when I walked into the Laurieston Bar and all of a sudden it was 6.30 pm so I ask Joe Clancy behind the bar to call me a taxi to take me to the Glencairn Club. My taxi arrives and takes me through the streets of the Gorbals that I once walked when I was a wean, and oh how the buildings have all changed (to me in my mind the tenements are still standing and it's hard to try and recognise where the streets once were). So the taxi goes by the Southern Necropolis Graveyard on Caledonia Rd and we're going past Fauldhouse Way, which used to be my street, although it was called Fauldhouse St back then, and I look at all these new houses that have been built in the Oatlands regeneration and I really just cannot take it all in. Then we pass by Shawfield Stadium and I'm glad that I can see it is still standing and then my taxi draws up outside the Glencairn Club at 7.00 pm. I walk in the door and there is Colin Mackie and his lovely wife, Elsie, to greet me.

Now the Glencairn Club has only a few of the bar staff there, and one of them is Mark Hughes, the son of the late Marie Hughes (God

Bless her) and we have a talk and I offer him my deepest condolences as the last time we had met at the Gorbals Reunion his mother had still been alive. Colin Mackie and Elsie have done a wonderful job in getting all the tables set up and there are street names of the old Oatlands laying on top of the tables which I think was a good idea, so you would have 'Polmadie Rd' on one table, one table with 'Roseberry St' on it and another and so on and so on. I looked for the table with the Fauldhouse St sign on it and just as I was going to sit down there, my pal, Billy Harvie and his lovely wife Liz, walked through the door, so we all sat down together and before you knew where you were, the hall was starting to fill up and I was looking out to see if I could spot anybody I knew.

Colin had come up with a good idea that was as people handed over their admission ticket, they received a name tag to stick on their jacket or dress, and then that way if you got talking to someone, then you would know them straight away and stopped you from wondering "Who the bloomin' hell am I speaking to?" I noticed Martin Curran straight away and he introduced me to his daughters and sons in law. Then out of the blue this lad walked over to me, it was only Robert (Rab) Fulton who I used to play with when we were weans in my back court and his brother William. Well you could have knocked me down with a feather. It was truly great meeting up with them after fifty four years and we had a good old talk.

Then another old school friend turned up, it was Mitchell Crombie, who had been in my primary school class and who was also our goalkeeper for Wee Bonnies football team and his lovely wife, Ann McCourt, who had actually been in our class too. Ann and Mitchell had married years later after leaving school, oh this reunion night was getting better all the time. Eamon Monaghan, whose ma and da's window faced our window in the back courts of our tenements was also there, and once again we had a good old talk.

I looked round the hall and it was pretty packed. I did get to speak to May Bishop Sweeney and Jean Shreenan and Mary Higgins and we had a quick wee bleather, then I spoke to Gerry Macaleavy and his fiancée, Irene then a quick word with Danny Sweeney and his lovely wife. In between speaking to everyone, Colin had organised a photo/slide show of how the old Oatlands of the tenement era looked and these were shown on a wall screen about six feet square.

Then the music started and people were getting up to dance but I'm afraid with me having arthritis in my knees, my dancing days are over, but it was great to see everyone enjoying themselves. I sat back down at my table with my pal Billy and his wife Liz and soon we were joined with Eddie Graham and his wife Brenda and we had a great old talk.

There were so many people there that it would have taken all night to speak to everyone but I was glad that I had the opportunity to speak to at least some of the people. The music played, the people danced and having a drink was the order of the night, while everyone seemed to be taking photos on their mobile phones. Altogether what a great turn out on the night.

Then it came to the raffle ticket draws for all the prizes that people had kindly donated on the night for the two charities, I had donated two copies of my books. One was my autobiography and the other my latest one "Gorbals and Oatlands". When people had won these I personally signed them for their goodselves and quite a few people had brought along a copy of my book "Gorbals and Oatlands" which they had previously bought and I was more than delighted to personally sign them.

It really was a great night especially meeting up with my friends from my soo side days when I was a wean. It was also great to meet up with my new friends too, that I had met on Facebook. I wonder what our parents and grandparents would have thought of all this computer and internet invention which has enabled us to reconnect with friends that we hadn't saw since our primary schooldays, they wouldn't have believed it possible. My pal Billy and his wife got picked up in their son's car outside of the Glencairn Club at gone midnight and very kindly gave me a lift back to my Eurostar Hostel in Jamaica St. We promised to keep in touch and after thanking them for making this a most enjoyable evening, I got the lift up to my room, put my head on the pillow and fell fast asleep (that Vodka is a great sleeping tablet).

The next day, being Sunday, I went to the Laurieston Bar and met up with Peter Mortimer at 1.00 pm in the afternoon and what a great five hours we shared. Peter has written quite a few books, not only about the Gorbals but of Glasgow's other areas too. I have read a few of them and they are most informative with plenty of photos taken by his friend Duncan McCallum. Peter also gives lectures and talks about Glasgow in general and his knowledge knows no bounds, what a great down to earth person he really is.

We had a great old talk (with a few drinks too) and it was great to be able to speak to someone so knowledgeable and we spoke of many aspects/topics covering the soo side and our childhoods. Peter was born in (or just off) Ballater St beside that fantastic looking building the U.C.B.S. Of course, we discussed our lives growing up in the tenements and everything that went with it. Then after a terrific afternoon discussing the soo side we knew as weans it was time for us call it a day. Peter had received a phone call on his mobile from his wife saying his dinner would be ready in an hour's time and so we parted company. I walked over to Wetherspoon's Pub in Jamaica St and had my Sunday dinner in there. What a fabulous day.

On the Tuesday I had agreed to meet up with members of the Facebook site "Bookworms" where people discuss what books they are reading and which ones they recommend for others to read. As I have stated before, I have always been an avid book reader ever since I joined the library in Mc Neil St all those years ago when I was a wean, and the "reading bug" has never left me, so I met up with Pauline Sim who founded the group and Diane Henderson, Martha Brindley (who wrote her brother Iain's life story).

Our meeting place was Wetherspoon's Pub in Jamaica St and by now the staff of the pub were getting used to seeing me there now (ha ha), so we had a great wee afternoon talking about books and life in general. Martha and myself signed each other's copies of our books, then Margaret Hillier joined our company which was great. Diane had to leave to attend to her children as they were due out of school and Pauline and Martha left as they had their train to catch, so this left Margaret and myself, but only for a brief moment as Manny Healy had just walked in the door, so we stayed for another hour and all together we had a great afternoon, and I think once again what a wonderful invention this internet and Facebook are.

The following day, Wednesday, I had promised to go out to Rutherglen to meet up with Norrie McNamee, he is in the "Glescapals" Facebook site just like me. I must have known and talked to Norrie for over five years and he is a very nice man indeed. One of his hobbies is photography and over the years he must have taken hundreds of photos of the Gorbals and Oatlands area's (plus other parts of Glasgow), and anytime that I need any photos for one of my books, then Norrie would always post them to me. In fact, I thank him in the acknowledgement pages of two of my books.

We met up in the Wetherspoon's pub (where else!!) in Main St, Rutherglen and it was great to finally meet up with the man who has helped me so much with photos over the years. Norrie is a very kind person and for a few hours we sat and took a walk down memory lane, and, of course, we got someone to take our photo. Then it was time to part company and I waited at the bus stop for the bus to take me back into Glasgow. As I was standing at the bus stop there, I looked round once more at Rutherglen and think to myself 'what a lovely wee town.'

My bus arrives and we pass by the Glencairn Club, Shawfield Stadium, Fauldhouse Way (my old street), the Southern Necropolis, Citizens Theatre and into Argyle St. I walk along the now pedestrianised section of it and enter St Enoch's Square and go into the "Square Peg " pub, which I now believe is called "Times Square" and have a few beers. When I come out again it still amazes me how much St Enoch's Square has changed over the years, and I still expect to see a bus draw up, as this used to be the bus terminus and taxi rank and I look at what used to be the subway entrance, that lovely sandstone building that looks a wee bit like a castle, and it's now a cafe/restaurant and I think "Oh where has the Glasgow gone that I used to know?"

I then go along Howard St and go into the Imperial Bar which is almost behind my Eurostar Hostel and sit down and have a few beers. This is the kind of Glasgow pub that I used to know before I left Glasgow in the late nineteen sixties to begin my travels. The barmaid always has a cheery word for you, and as you stand at the bar you always seem to strike up a conversation with the person next to you. After having a few beers I go to the K.F.C (Kentucky Fried Chicken) which now stands where Boots the Chemist/'Dizzy Corner' used to stand and get a take away meal for my hostel room and have a night in my room watching a bit of TV and trying to keep fresh for the following day, when I am due to meet up with a good few friends from the "Glasgow Banter" Facebook site and I think to myself, how it's really good to have so many friends nowadays, and all thanks to the internet and Facebook.

So it's Thursday morning and I get up and have a shower and shave and leave my hostel and walk round the corner to the St Enoch Square shopping mall and have my breakfast in one of the many eating places there. I then have a walk up to George Square and have a walk around it, then I go back down Queen St and go into Tam Shepard's joke shop and buy a lime green wig, as I always joke to my Glasgow banter friends that I wear a wig, and as I have promised to sing them a wee song later that day when we meet in Wetherspoon's, this will hopefully add a bit of spice to my singing act.

I meet up with my Facebook friends from the 'Glasgow Banter' site in the Wetherspoon's Pub in Jamaica St as Christine Thomson, one of our members, has booked a room at the back of the pub for us from 12.00 noon until 4.00 pm in the afternoon. I was the first there at 11.30 am and ordered a pint while waiting for all my friends to arrive.

By 1.00 pm most of the people had arrived and once again it's great to be able to sit face to face with people (as opposed to sending messages). I had met a few of the 'Banters' before when I was up in Glasgow the previous year, and that time we met up in the Hootenanny Pub in St Enoch's Square, but there were more people here today. Was that because I had promised to sing a song? (ha ha).

Well we were all having a great old gab and exchanging stories, some of us having a drink and some drinking tea, actually there were eleven girls who turned up that day. Gina, the 2 Ellens, Eileen S Stones, Annabell, Moyra, Mary, Grace, Eileen Stewart, Christine and Anne and what a brilliant gathering and great conversation we all had. Then at 3.00 pm I sang my wee song. I stood up and put on my lime green wig and started to sing a wee song called "I'm a Rambler, I'm a gambler, I'm a long way from home" and I think the whole of the pub was listening. I couldn't have been too bad as the manager never asked me to leave!! I think all the 'Banter' girls liked it!!

Then out of the blue and completely unexpected, all the 'Banter' girls presented me with a bottle of Glenfiddich Malt Whisky with my name on the label. What a very kind gesture and it took me by compete surprise, and I felt very humbled by this kind gift. All the girls said it was in appreciation of my weekly Friday poem that I post on the 'Banter' site and a few short stories to give us all a laugh. In addition, a few of the girls brought along a copy of one or two of my books and I was more than happy to personally sign them.

It's surprising when you're enjoying yourself that the time flies in but all of a sudden it's 4.00 pm and a few of the girls start to leave and I say goodbye to them all and thank them all for taking the time to turn up and meet me (and the others), and thanks to our Christine Thomson who took the trouble and booked the room for us in the pub. Now the time is almost 5.30 pm and I leave myself, all this drinking every day, while enjoyable, is catching up with me. I say my farewell to the girls and go over the street to my hostel, go to bed and fall fast asleep, oh what a great afternoon!!

Next day, Friday, I get up and shower and shave, have a full Scottish breakfast in Wetherspoon's pub and take a walk at lunch time to have a slow beer in the Laurieston Bar. One thing I like about the Laurieston is that it always has a few daily newspapers for its customers to read. I sit there just sipping a pint of beer and having a good old talk with John Clancy, who, along with his brother James and family run the pub. I don't want to drink too much as I'm meeting up with Carol Connelly, her sister Sandra and their friend Lorraine McIvor in Sharkey's Bar later that night. I only have two beers and take a walk back to my hostel and lay down on top of the bed. I leave my hostel at 6.30 pm that evening and take a slow walk along Clyde St heading towards Sharkey's Pub.

As I pass by Clyde St I think back to years ago when one side of the street was the bus terminus for all the red buses and I sometimes had caught the red bus going to Neilston (but getting off at Nitshill). In my late teens I used to have a pint in a pub called the Vintner's in Clyde St before boarding that bus, but sadly with the passing of time the red buses have gone and so has the Vintner's Pub. I wonder how many people just like me have returned to their native city and stood in awe at all the changes that have happened to Glasgow since they have left. I'm sure that they must be amazed too, and it does take you a while to come to terms with all the changes.

Anyway, I walk up to the Victoria Bridge and cross over it and make my way to Sharkey's Bar. I'm starting to get to know my way better in the soo side now as I don't get lost so muc!! I walk into Sharkey's just after 7.00 pm and the first person I see is Norah Greene and we sit down and have a natter (I had met Norah the previous year when I was home). Norah's local pub is the Pig and Whistle in McNeil St but she kindly has made her way here to have a drink with me. Next person to come into the pub is Lorraine White who I had met before too and then the '3 Gorbals Girls Out and

About' Carol, Sandra and Lorraine turn up, so we all go through to the lounge bar where there is more seating.

We all sit down and then David (Davie) Scott turns up and our company is getting larger and it really is great to see them all. Raymond Shannon (who I had also previously met) and Carol Connelly's mother, Alice, comes in and joins our company. Once again, what a great night we are all having, talking about all the old times and the up to date times too, plus some of the girls are going up to play records on the juke box as the selection of old pop music hits are really good. Our company is getting that big now we have taken up two seating areas in the lounge and then Maggie Steedman McKay joins our company.

Maggie and myself have been promising to meet up for ages and tonight we finally did. Maggie had left Glasgow just like me way back in the late sixties and went down to Wales to live and work but has now returned back home to live, so we had a great auld talk. Margaret Lyons and her friend (who's name escapes me at the moment, sorry) joined up with us as did Susan Anderson Knox and her husband. Molly Dooley also joined and I was busy trying to go round everyone and have a word with them all, I'm sorry if I have left anyone's name out or didn't get to speak to them on the night.

I have to thank everyone for taking the time to come and meet up with me on the night, it really was a fabulous time and Sharkey's is a very nice pub and so are all the staff behind the bar. Thanks everyone for making this night a most enjoyable one. I walked the short distance back to my hostel and once again fell fast asleep.

Next day my nephew Davie was coming in from Airdrie to meet up with me and catch up with all the news. Once again we made a meeting for Wetherspoon's Pub in Jamaica St and I think that the Wetherspoon's Pub staff think that I have got shares in the place (ha ha). Davie had just returned from a holiday in Tenerife with his lovely wife Lynn and had a terrific sun tan, and my mind goes back to when I was twenty years old and working in London waiting on my sister Jeanette to give birth to Davie ,and I think "Where have all the years gone?" They seem to have just flown in.

So Davie and myself have a good old talk (oh and a few drinks too) then it's time for Davie to get his train back to Airdrie and for me to go and have a lay down on the hostel bed. I did, and then went out for the last hour in the Imperial pub in Howard St, just round the corner form my hostel.

I get up the following morning, shower, shave and then as it's my last day of my holiday back home in Glasgow, I take a slow walk along Argyle St then the Trongate and as I stand looking over at Glasgow Cross and that big tower clock at the junction of High Street, Gallowgate, London Road, Saltmarket and Trongate, I think what would life have been like for me if I hadn't travelled and stayed in Glasgow and married my girlfriend Rena? Who knows, but I think I was always meant to travel and overall I can be happy with the way my life has turned out with my own daughters and grand weans in London. Sure I made a few mistakes along the way but then again I'm only human.

Monday morning arrives and I make my way to the Central Station and catch the train back to London and think what a truly wonderful last ten days it has been back in Glasgow, these are more memories of the soo side for me to remember. I get back to my wee flat in London and say "Right Danny boy, time to start saving up for my trip back to Glasgow next year."

Epilogue

Now as I look back on my soo side memories it is with great fondness and hope that you, the reader, have enjoyed my trip down memory lane. Can it really be all that long ago that what I have mentioned has happened? I look at my school-class photo (when I was five years old) that hangs up in my living room wall and when I look at it I always say "Well class mates, how did your life go? Mine was brilliant."

Treasured memories of my growing up in the south side of Glasgow, the love of my parents and grandparents, all my pals that I played with in the back courts of the tenements and getting clatty dirty but always being happy. Going to primary school and loving that wee bottle of milk that we all got but not really liking the school lessons as all I wanted to do was play football at playtime with my pals.

Then moving onto Junior then Senior Secondary Schools and loving going to France on a school-exchange holiday, holding Elizabeth's hand on the train and experiencing wine for the first time while wearing my first long trousered suit at thirteen years old.

All what we got up to as weans growing up, all the street games we used to play and being loved unconditionally by our parents and neighbour's alike. Days out going midgie raking or heading to Gorbals swimming baths, or going to Richmond Park for a day out, while remembering getting threepence worth of scrapings from Greasy Peters fish and chip shop. Buying second hand comic's from Dirty Maggies shop and the joy of going to the picture hoose with your pals and a hundred other things we used to do when growing up in that era of the old tenements, and last, but not least, that wonderful close knit community spirit that we all shared.

Then the disaster of the back of my tenement collapsing and all my family and me being shipped out to one of the new housing schemes that were being built on the outskirts of Glasgow, and the sheer feeling of abandonment at having to leave the soo side where I had spent my formative years.

Starting work and making my way in life but always returning to my roots, meeting my girlfriend Rena and those wonderful Friday nights in the Clelland bar music lounge. I close my eyes and can still see the band playing their guitars and that magic atmosphere. I will never forget those wonderful memories.

Leaving to work in London and other countries when I had finished my five year apprenticeship as a bricklayer, never returning to live or work (sadly) in Glasgow again, but going home on holiday and the new year to see my ma and da.

Learning to use a computer when I was sixty two years old and being able to "talk" to people on the Gorbals and Oatlands on Facebook sites and seeing photos of my old school and other buildings in the soo side that I never in my wildest dreams thought I would ever see again. Then when ma and da passed away, making myself a promise to return to look at the old place after an absence of forty five years.

Well I did return but I could hardly recognise the place where I had been brought up with the exception of the Southern Necropolis Graveyard on Caledonia Rd and St Francis' Church. Meeting up with some of my old school pals (via Facebook) and meeting them in the flesh, how tremendous, and also meeting up with my new friends form the Gorbals and Oatlands, and what great people they all are.

I now make a yearly holiday trip back to Glasgow and meet up with all my friends and look forward to this with the greatest of pleasure. My last book "Gorbals and Oatlands" has been published and I donated all the royalty payments to go to the upkeep of the Southern Necropolis Graveyard on Caledonia Rd, this was just my way of saying thank you to the soo side for my wonderful childhood and upbringing.

I would like to personally thank everyone who has taken the time to read this book of mine Emah Roo because whether you spell it backwards or read it backwards it translates to Emah Roo - Oor Hame.

God Bless.

The Fair Fortnight

For the last two weeks in July, most of Glasgow folk said goodbye.
Going away fur the Fair and hoping that the weather would be dry.

Lots of Gorbals people went to Rothsey or Dunoon wae a big smile.
While others went to Blackpool for two weeks along its Golden mile.

Everyone seemed to be so happy, we had money and it wiz the fair.
Ye cood go to Billy Butlin's holiday camp just opened up doon in Ayr.

My ma and da took us tae Saltcoats, we travelled there by the train.
Then a new thing called a package holiday took folks over to Spain.

Changing your money to Pesetas aff to Espana withoot even a ruffle.
Where you drank San Miguel aw night and done the soo side shuffle.

Oh life wiz great fun fur the Fair fortnight, suntanned as dark as hide.
But all too soon it wiz over as we all travelled back to the old soo side.

Back to the auld Sunny Gorbals, by boat, car, train or even the plane.
We knew we were aw back hame because it wiz lashin doon wae rain.

Queen o the Steamie

She was known as Queen o the Steamie her name Agnes McSweeney.
Filling her pram up wae washing, shirts, skirts and a dirty auld peeney.

Livin in an old tenement hoose two stairs up in busy Cumberland Street.
Always first to finish her washing, oor Agnes she wiz never wance beat.

Before she left the steamie, she wid share the gossip wae other maws.
Did ye hear aboot oor big Ella living in sin oot by in sunny Pollokshaws.

Or what aboot free and easy Isa, who's new baby she's called it Davie.
How can that be her man's been away fur 2 years in the Merchant Navy.

So Agnes done it once again left aw the other washin wummen standing.
That's it fur another week, as she pushed her pram up ontae her landing.

She went back in her hoose, resting her feet while drinking a cup of tea.
Thinking because I left the steamie early, are they gossiping aboot me?

This was a century ago now kitchens hiv washing machines so dreamy.
It's a long time now since Agnes McSweeney was Queen o the Steamie.

Gorbals Cross

When I think of the Gorbals clearance, it leaves me at a loss.
Not only were the houses demolished but also Gorbals Cross.

Traffic was always busy, all along Norfolk and Ballater Street.
Shops were everywhere, going fur the messages wiz a treat.

Up Gorbals St you had the baths where we'd all go for a swim.
Then after go to the Hot Peanut man, didn't us weans love him?

Round Gorbals Cross you had oh so many pubs, to enjoy a jar.
Too many pubs to name so I'll jist say Doyle's and Benny's Bar.

Then stood the Citizens Theatre, the Palace Cinema next door.
With the Princess Cafe and chip shops, ye coodny ask fur more.

But as I say this has all gone now, no more are people meeting.
And after being away over 45 years I looked and felt like greetin.

In progress's name Gorbals Cross, was destroyed whit a shame.
For with its destruction, oor generation will never feel the same.

The Coalman

From the far off end of Oatlands, all the way over up to Eginton Toll.
Came Jackson's Coal Merchant's lorry, with hunners a bags of coal.

From your tenement windae lookin below ,the coalman wiz standing
You'd shout down two bags fur Mrs Wilson up on the second landing.

Opening the wooden bunker in your lobby, closing the doors a must.
Cos when the coal wiz dumped ye coodny see fur aw the bloody dust.

The coalman stood there in your lobby black with coal fae head to toe.
After paying him he'd rejoin his lorry, and off to the next street he'd go.

Jackson's used to have horses and carts before lorryies joined his fleet.
The horses were kept in the pen in between Sandyfaulds and Moffat St.

Also in the soo side you had no chance of missin Jackson's coal patrol.
Cos the guy on the back of the lorry, burst his lungs shouting "Cahole".

Jacksons Coal Merchants are in the past, their coal we no longer desire.
Nowadays we have central heating or a new thing called an electric fire.

Fish and Chips

Today you can have an Indian or Chinese food in a silver foiled-tray.
When I was a wean the Fish n Chip shop wiz oor fast food take away.

A special Fish Supper wrapped up in newspaper, made us aw swoon
Wae a bottle of Irn Bru or American cream soda tae wash it aw doon.

Now some people in the soo side would say Ann's Fry passed the test
But we all have different opinion's, of what Fish n Chip shop wiz best.

Aye some say it wiz Mario's but it wiz really hard for all of us to decide.
So who knows what the best Fish n Chip shop was in aw the soo-side.

Friday night wiz the main night of the week fur all us Fish n Chip eaters.
And there used to be a mile long queue outside of auld Greasy Peter's.

Who remembers those Battered Fritters, oh they really did hit the mark.
People fae Oatlands used Giovanis chipper opposite of Richmond Park.

I don't like the home delivery of Curry's n Pizzas to tell ye the honest truth.
I'd rather be queuing ootside o the Fish n Chip shop slaverin at the mooth.

Stairheid Toilet

Can you remember years ago when the old tenements were standing.
To go to the toilet you'd hiv to walk downstairs to the stairheid landing.

There were three families who would share oor toilet, as off you'd go.
But if there wiz an emergency, then under the bed we kept the old po.

You'd try and announce your presence, by whistling like a wee budgie.
And if you heard a cough then you knew somebody wiz in the cludgie.

Waiting your turn to go to the stairheid toilet really wiz a common thing.
And you prayed that there wiz newspaper hingin fae that bit of o string.

Winter times cood be dark so you took a lit candle, naw ye wurrny vain.
Then run like mad back up the stairs after you'd pulled the lavvy chain.

Then oor tenements got demolished we got moved to housin schemes.
We had a bath and an inside toilet, it was the answer to all oor dreams.

But I'll never forget the stairheid toilet for as long as my old heart beats.
As we repose in our luxury en suite bathrooms, with heated toilet seats.

Saltcoats By The Sea

For two weeks in the summer, we had a holiday feeling so rare.
Cos most people in the soo side went away fur the Glesga Fair.

Ma and da took oor family on the bus oer tae the Central Station.
I was burstin with excitement cause Saltcoats wiz oor destination.

We stayed in a boarding house just five minutes walk fae the sea.
There wiz ma and da , my big sister, and my wee granny and me.

Every day wiz a beach day ma,da and granny would sit an natter.
Granda's with rolled up trooser legs, wid paddle in the sea watter.

Breathing in that salt sea air every day, it was for us a magic treat.
Wizny half a big change fae Caledonia Road or Cumberland Street.

During the day a big ice cream, and at night times a poke of chips.
Even jist thinking about it nowadays still has me smacking my lips.

But soon oor holiday was over and it was goodbye from you n me.
I coodny wait to tell my soo side pal's, aboot Saltcoats by the sea

Old Money

I was brought up in the soo side before we had this decimalisation.
We all used pounds, shillings and pence throughout all the nation.

Remember the old wooden threepenny bit or the auld silver tanner.
The farthing had gone, but a penny bought you all sorts of manner.

Then we had the two bob florin, the half crown couldn't be neater.
Ye coodny forget the shilling piece as it dropped into oor gas meter.

Next we had the paper money, and there was wan that got my vote.
You know the wan I am talking aboot, yes that old red ten bob note.

Then we moved to higher denomination and this really wiz a caper.
T'was the old white Fiver, it unfolded to the size of a newspaper.

Accepting those wee smaller fivers also ten pound notes with thanks.
Hardly ever seeing an English note, we had so many Scottish banks.

Nowadays we hiv a one pound coin and a 50 pence that looks funny.
Oh how I do long for the old days when we had old fashioned money.

Primary School

Who remembers the days when we went to our Primary School.
When we learned our times tables and used an old wooden rule.

We made our way to school each morning trying never to be late.
Because after nine o'clock the school Janny closed the front gate.

Ma took ye to school on your first day, looking on wae great pride.
This happened in schools aw o'er Glasgow, no jist in the soo side.

Sitting in your seat listening and did everything that you were telt.
Cos if you didny then the teacher would give you six of the belt.

Wiz plenty of schools in the soo side, to cover every faith and Ilk.
Sharin wan thing in common, that wee third of a pint bottle of milk.

Some of us liked learning lessons but I coodny be bothered at aw.
Waiting to hear the playtime bell so I cood run oot and play fitbaw,

Primary School days were magic, their memories will never cease.
My best recollection wiz at playtime staunin eating mah jeely piece.

Christmas Past

Here's to the memory of our Christmas's past as we aw think back in joy.
Oor ma n da never had that much money, we were happy to get any toy.

This is the way it was back then, and some people think that it's shocking.
But us weans were over the moon to get an orange in oor Xmas stocking.

Now if ma had any money to spare she took us oer to the toon as a treat.
And who could forget queuing up for Santa's grotto in Lewis's in Argyle St.

On Christmas Eve us weans coodny get to sleep waitin fur Santa to come.
Never thinking for a minute, how the big man got down oor chimney lum.

As the tenement windaes froze over, and the snow heavily started to fall.
Us boys and lassies fell asleep hoping that Santa would be good to us all.

No matter what toys we got from Santa we were so happy we cood greet.
Then ran doon the stairs to show aff oor presents to oor pals in the street.

This is how it was years ago as we celebrated the birth of Jesus our King.
Our community-spirit wiz brilliant, we had nothing but we had everything.

Sore Heid

What's yer cure for a hangover as I think that I've really tried them aw.
I have tried the cures told to me by my granda, granny, and my maw.

I remember my granny saying, take an Askit powder with some mulk.
She swore by it so much that she would order boxes of Askits in bulk.

But that never seemed to work for me Oh Lord what can I honestly do.
My Uncle said, stick yer heid under the tap, and hiv a glass of Irn Bru.

Saturday mornings when I have a hangover, well I wish that I wiz deid.
What can I take to ease this pain and get rid of this bloomin sore heid.

I have pals who don't drink and they get headaches jist as bad as mine.
They take an Abdine, the white then blue sachet and they then feel fine.

We know the guidelines for alcohol but sometimes we don't stop to think.
The reality of it hits you the next morning wae yer heid stuck in the sink.

I'm never gonny drink again my heid is thumping and my eyes are agog
But wait a minute haud yer horses, I'm jist gonny have a hair of the dog.

Smog

Do you remember the smog attacks we had, it really wiz a disgrace.
You could taste it in your mooth, so you tied a scarf a roon yer face.

The buses aw crawled at a snail's pace it took you hours to get hame.
It was the smoke fae the factory chimneys that really wiz all to blame.

This was the 1950's in Glasgow it was murder polis and that is a fact.
Pea soup thick smog was so bad Parliament passed the clean air act.

It didn't deter the young soccer players in the street, no wan bit ataw.
Running aboot with scarves over their mooth's, trying to see the fitbaw.

People's chesty coughs wiz murder as doctors listened to their moans.
Power stations moved outside the city, we got new "smokeless zones."

Electric fires wid take over, no more burning coal, now you'd burn coke.
Soon the air was getting cleaner thank God, cos that smog wiz no joke.

This story of the smog attacks happened years ago, as my story goes.
When us Glaswegian's couldn't see a foot in front of our bloomin nose.

The Co-op Dividend Number

Can you remember the Co-op of all those years gone by so long.
You got messages fur yer ma, and never got the number wrong.

Your ma told you her divvy number from when you were a wean.
It wiz drilled into your memory and forever imprinted in yer brain.

You first heard your ma's number, as she rattled it off with pride.
As she dragged you to every Co-op shop, in the whole soo side.

I remember standing in the Co-op as the money wiz put in a cup.
And it whizzed its way to the cashier, seated in the office high up.

The divvy pay-oot was fantastic, as you got it paid oot every year.
Made your ma dead happy, buying her weans a ton of new gear.

Ma's divvy number still gets used each week but in a different way.
The numbers I use for the lottery and hope I'll be lucky some day.

When we meet St Peter at the Pearly Gates, he'll say with a grin.
If ye canny remember yer ma's divvy number yer jist no getting in.

Central Station

How many times have we stood there, catchin a train to oor destination.
But things have changed so much over the years to the Central Station.

I remember when it was steam engines and Porters almost everywhere.
Folks all lining up wae suitcases, as they went away fur the Glesga Fair.

The Shell monument on the concourse, a meeting place fur oh so many.
With a wee slot near to the top, if you felt you wanted to drop in a penny.

Wae big signs advertising Askit or Beecham's Powders, urging one a day.
Changed days noo because they advertise aw that fast food take away.

The "Heilan-mans umberella" jist at the corner of Hope and Argyle Street.
A great rendezvous place for all the Highland men to congregate n meet.

There's always a buzz about the Central Station, people going to and fro.
And it was here as a young man, that I left for London half a century ago.

Now every time I return home to Glasgow, I still get that feeling of elation.
Bolts of electricity charging through my body, as I land in Central Station.

Glasgow Revisited

I saved up for my holiday all year round, Glasgow was my destination.
And electric charges ran up my legs, as I landed in the Central Station.

First night I'd a few pints in the Laurieston Bar then off to my hotel bed.
The following day I met a rake of friends, gathering in the Brazen Head.

Oh what a buzz to be in the soo-side again, and with all my ain folk too.
The Glencairn twas brilliant as we gathered fur the Oatlands reunion do.

The tenements we grew up in are now gone, their memory is still sweet.
Argyle St is nearly aw pedestrianised but there's beggars on every street.

I met wae loads of Facebook friends, in Wetherspoon's jist over the toon.
My pal Peter Mortimer n me talked about the next Gorbals book out soon.

What a ten day holiday I had fae early morn to when the moon wiz bright
And how we all laughed in Sharkey's Bar, on my second last Friday night.

Bein back hame in Glasgow wae my ain folk, was a holiday so well spent.
But drank so much I've to detox for a month as I climb into an oxygen tent.